Soviet Elite Attitudes Since Stalin

Merrill Political Science Series

Under the Editorship of
John C. Wahlke

Department of Political Science
The University of Iowa

Soviet Elite Attitudes Since Stalin

Milton C. Lodge

University of Iowa

Charles E. Merrill Publishing Co.
A Bell & Howell Company
Columbus, Ohio

Standard Book Number 675-09435-6

Library of Congress Catalog Card Number: 73-86335

1 2 3 4 5 6 / 74 73 72 71 70 69

Printed in the United States of America

ACKNOWLEDGMENTS

The data for this study were collected at the Institute for the Study of the USSR, Munich, Germany, in the winter of 1965-66, funded by a fellowship from the University of Michigan Center for Russian and East European Studies, and a travel grant from the University of Michigan Horace H. Rackham School of Graduate Studies. Both institutions serve the student of Soviet politics well.

Several people deserve special thanks. Edward Crowley provided me with free access to the fine library and facilities of the Munich Institute. I am most grateful to the coders for their cooperation, hard work, splendid lunchtime conversations, and memorable end-of-project party. Their dedication to this study lends it credence.

Constructive critics of the manuscript number in the dozens. Citing only those who saved me from grave errors, I thank William Welsh and William Zimmerman. Because the study of Soviet politics is, or should be, a part of political science, I owe a special debt of gratitude to my departmental colleagues at the University of Iowa. I also extend my appreciation to the editors of the *Midwest Journal of Political*

Science and the *American Political Science Review* for permission to incorporate material which originally appeared in the two journals.

While it is true that numerous people helped make this a better book, I alone must acknowledge responsibility for its failings. I accept this responsibility, but I believe that the Soviet leaders themselves should accept their share for making research on Soviet politics so very difficult.

Finally, I dedicate this book to my wife Janet. Not simply for her moral support, common sense, typing and editing, but because I am sure that whatever the critics' choice—whether excessive praise or damning rejection—she will question quietly their intellect.

Contents

1 Introduction

This study is a comparative analysis of five Soviet elites—
the full-time Party functionaries (the *apparatchiki*), and four
specialist elites: the economic administrators, the military,
the literary intelligentsia, and the legal profession. By content
analyzing representative periodicals for each elite, data are
collected on elite attitudes toward the Soviet political system.
The overall goal is to determine the extent to which the *apparatchiki* dominate the political process, more specifically, to
measure the degree to which the specialist elites manifest the
attitudinal orientations of active participants in the post-
Stalin period.

To ground this study in a theoretical framework, analytical
categories and hypotheses are derived in part from Brzezinski
and Huntington's *Political Power: USA/USSR*.[1] Synoptically,
models of political systems may be built by reducing to essentials the mode of interaction between the regime and
society. A key variable in analyzing this interaction be-

---

[1] Zbigniew Brzezinski and Samuel Huntington, *Political Power:
USA/USSR* (New York, The Viking Press, 1964), Chaps. 1-4.

1

tween the superstructure and base is the role and efficacy of societal groups in the political process. Following this approach a descriptive continuum may be set up for classifying political systems. Near one end of the continuum are ideological systems (e.g., the USSR), near the other, instrumental systems (e.g., the United States). In instrumental systems the relationship between the political and social system is characterized by the "access and interaction" of societal groups in the political system, in ideological systems by the "control and manipulation" of groups by the top leaders of the ruling party. As an ideological system the Soviet political system is distinguished by the dominance of the Party apparat in the political process. Societal groups are infiltrated, controlled, and manipulated by the *apparatchiki* and thereby denied a participatory role in policy-making and implementation.

Brzezinski, along with a growing number of Western scholars, notes some degree of Soviet systematic change in the post-Stalin period, arguing that the Party apparat, while still dominant in the political arena, is being forced to tolerate greater specialist elite participation in the political process. To gain a measure of the extent of change along the continuum toward a more instrumental (i.e., elite participatory) political system, attitudinal data are collected on two operational indicators of Party-elite relations: one, the level of specialist elite participation, the other, the degree of elite group consciousness. Trends toward a more instrumental system would be indicated by a dual development over time: (1) the specialist elites must articulate a set of participatory beliefs and values which make them attitudinal co-participants with the Party in policy-making, and (2) the specialist elites must manifest a sense of group identity which is both distinct from that of the Party *apparatchiki* and supportive of elite participation.[2]

The ideological-instrumental continuum may be portrayed as an attitudinal field ranging from Party Dominance on the ideological side of the continuum to Specialist-Elite Participation on the instrumental side, with the middle ground corresponding to joint Party-specialist elite participation. Two sets of categories are designed to generate data suitable for plotting the elites on the attitudinal continuum.

Indicators of elite group consciousness are developed through six nominal categories which tap a set of the beliefs, values, and policy preferences of the elites. The categories are as follows:

[2] One word of caution. All the data in this study tap elite articulated attitudes, not political behavior in the ministries, committees, and offices of the Kremlin. When we speak about changes since Stalin we are dealing solely with attitudinal changes, changes in Soviet elite perspectives and values. Assumed, of course, is a positive correlation between articulated attitudes and political behavior.

Do the elites perceive themselves as groups, and are they perceived by others as a group?

Who is responsible for elite socialization?

What is the role of the Party?

What should be the role of the Party?

How should resources be allocated?

How should the population be mobilized?

The aim of the policy categories is to gain a measure of the extent to which the elites constitute attitudinally distinct groups. Answers are sought to the questions: How, when, why do the specialist elites differ from the Party *apparatchiki?* Do the specialist elites share a set of beliefs and values which distinguish them from the full-time Party functionary? In sum, do the elites manifest the attitudinal makeup of analytically distinct groups?

The second set of categories focuses on the development of participatory attitudes:

Who is responsible for policy-making?

Who should be responsible for policy-making?

Who is responsible for local decision-making?

Who should be responsible for local decision-making?

How are policy recommendations justified?[3]

The questions asked: Do the specialist elites *perceive* themselves as attitudinal participants in the Soviet political process? Do they *aspire* to a co-participant role with the *apparatchiki?* Are the specialist elites developing a set of participatory attitudes which tends to undermine the dominance of the Party apparat in policy making and implementation?

This hypothesized relationship between the development of group consciousness and participatory attitudes in the post-Stalin period may be plotted on the ideological-instrumental continuum, as in Figure 1.

In this hypothetical situation the Soviet political system is becoming increasingly instrumental over time (T): both the level of specialist

---

[3] Each of the participatory categories is scaled:
1.0 Party participation solely
2.0 Party participation primarily
3.0 Joint Party-specialist participation
4.0 Specialist participation primarily
5.0 Specialist participation solely

The Soviet Political System

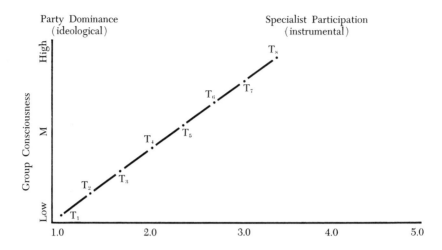

Fig. 1.   The Ideological-Instrumental Continuum

elite participatory attitudes and the degree of group consciousness increase. With 3.0 reflecting relatively equal Party-specialist elite participation, at T_1 (1952) the political system is Party Dominant (specialist
elite participation and group consciousness are low, the *apparatchiki*
are dominant); at T_8 (1965) the system is in the instrumental range
(specialist elite participatory scores reach the co-participation range
and the level of elite group consciousness is high).

Within the Party's espoused values for the "transition to communism," the knowledge and skills of specialists, it is reasoned, are indis-
pensable. "No single strategic elite," writes Suzanne Keller, "can today
know all there is to be known, and none can perform all the functions
involved in social leadership."[4] If it is true that the *apparatchiki* and
specialists are becoming increasingly interdependent, what, from the
Party's perspective, would be the ideal Party-specialist elite relationship? Ruling out either polar extreme as systematically dysfunctional,
a tentative "mix" may be a "mini-max" position in which the maximum

---

[4] *Beyond the Ruling Class: Strategic Elites in Modern Society* (New York: Random House, 1963), p. 70. The five elites in this study generally conform to Keller's
concept of strategic elites and fulfill the expectation that elite participation will increase over time. See too, Robert A. Dahl, *Who Governs: Democracy and Power in
an American City* (New Haven: Yale University Press, 1961), for a discussion of
elite pluralism in systems where political resources (e.g., knowledge and skills) are
dispersed and broadly distributed.

degree of specialist participation is tolerable which still allows for *apparatchiki* dominance in the political arena. With 3.0 corresponding to Party-specialist co-participation, the Party's optimal position would be in the 2.5-2.9 range where the *apparatchiki* could best capitalize on specialist elite participation without surrendering control.

I. Research Method

Western analyses of Soviet politics must, of necessity, rely heavily on published sources. Both the totalitarian and Kremlinological models typically portray Soviet communication channels as being monopolistically controlled by the central Party *apparat*. Rejecting both approaches this project assumes that the Soviet specialist elites—due to their strategic role in society—enjoy sufficient leeway in the system to articulate a distinctive range of beliefs and values in their specialist journals.

Soviet spokesmen grudgingly acknowledge and Western analyses have demonstrated that specialist journals are vehicles for the limited articulation of elite attitudes.[5] Representing a functional sphere of activity in the political system, specialist journals primarily perform an *instrumental* role—authors, as experts, elaborate on policies within their sphere of competence, suggest ways and means for improving implementation, mobilize support, and most important of all, criticize shortcomings. The overwhelming majority of sampled articles are achievement oriented, that is, they are chiefly concerned with questions of how best to fulfill the plan, increase efficiency and overcome weaknesses.

Within this orientation authors are predominantly concerned with specifics: a manager of a textile factory in Petropavlosk argues that Party interference in the running of the plant resulted in decreased production; a Marshal complains that criticism of company commanders at Party meetings undermines military authority and reduces troop

---

[5] Soviet references to this problem are numerous. See e.g., the authoritative editorial titled "Concerning Discussions in Scholarly Journals," in *Kommunist*, No. 7, 1955, which, after stating that Marxism-Leninism must be the "essential" framework within which specialist discussion should take place, bemoans the fact that scholarly articles "often" bypass Party formulas and all too frequently attempt "to reverse fundamental theses of the Party." For a general discussion of the increasing leeway for instrumental criticism in the post-Stalin period, see Sidney Ploss, *Conflict and Decision-Making in Soviet Russia* (Princeton: Princeton University Press, 1965), Chap. 1. A quantitative analysis comparing Soviet elite values manifested in journals is found in Robert Angell's "Social Values of Soviet and American Elites," and J. David Singer's "Social Values and Foreign Policy Attitudes of Soviet and American Elites," *Journal of Conflict Resolution* VIII, 4 (December 1964), pp. 329-491.

morale; a jurist warns that a Central Committee decree calling for the exemplary punishment of "parasites" undercuts the Party's campaign to strengthen socialist law; Tvardovsky, while editor-in-chief of *Novy mir,* favorably comments on "truthfulness" in literature, while Khrushchev rails against the young writers' emphasis on "decadent" themes. In sum, although specialist journals are rarely vehicles for an open and direct confrontation with the Party, specialist attitudes are articulated through instrumental proposals and criticism—within the Party's espoused values of productivity, efficiency and "communism"—without overtly challenging the Party's role in policy integration. In the Soviet context, rejection of the Party's integrative role is opposition, elite participation in the formulation and implementation of specific policies is politics. Direct opposition is rare, politics is ubiquitous. With the decline of terror in the post-Stalin period, controversies are no longer "zero-sum games."

The elites

For each elite, "representative" periodical(s) were selected for content analysis:

The Party *Apparat*	*Kommunist* (Communist)
	Partiinaya zhizn (Party Life)
The Economic Elite	*Voprosy ekonomiki* (Problems of Economics)
	Ekonomicheskaya gazeta (Economic Gazette)
The Military	*Krasnaya zvezda* (Red Star)
The Legal Profession	*Sovetskoye gosudarstvo i pravo* (Soviet State and Law)
	Sovetskaya yustitsia (Soviet Justice)
The Literary Elite	*Oktyabr* (October)
	Literaturnaya gazeta (Literary Gazette)
	Novy mir (New World)

The sample

To satisfy the definitional requirement of objectivity in content analysis, systematic sampling procedures are required.

1. The unit of analysis is the article. Articles in the sample were chosen from the periodicals on the basis of a quota sample. The issues from each periodical were selected at intervals so as to cover the

entire year and avoid the inclusion of any one period, e.g., avoiding every December issue of journals or Monday issue of newspapers. From the selected issue only the lead article, the first signed article, was coded. (In newspapers the lead article is the first signed article in the upper left-hand corner of page two.)

2. The unit of enumeration, what is being coded and counted, is the major theme of a paragraph. When clearly articulating one position in one category, the major theme could be coded once and only once.

3. The size of the sample is equal for each elite each year, 600 paragraphs per elite for each of the eight sampled years—1952, 1953, 1955, 1957, 1959, 1961, 1963, and 1965—a yearly sample of 3,000 paragraphs (600 paragraphs × 5 elites) for a total study sample of 24,000 paragraphs (3,000 paragraphs per year × 8 years).

Reliability

Reliability tests were administered to establish a presumption of objectivity. Twenty-five percent of all sampled articles were recoded by a second coder working independently of the first.[6] The articles included in the reliability test were selected by means of an "accidental sample," i.e., chosen randomly for each journal each year. The formula for testing reliability is:

$$\frac{\text{Total number of agreements}}{\substack{\text{Total number of paragraphs} \\ \text{in the article}}} = \text{percentage of reliability}$$

The total study reliability is statistically significant at 89.4 percent.

---

[6] See Instructions to Coders, Appendix A, and The Coders, Appendix B.

PART ONE

2 Elite Participatory Attitudes in the Post-Stalin Political System

The Soviet political system—when conceived as an ideological system—is characterized by Party apparat dominance in the political arena. One measure of trends toward an instrumental political system would be the development of elite participatory attitudes.

I. On Policy-Making

Question 1: Over time do the specialist elites increasingly describe themselves as participants in the policy-making process?

In operational terms Party primacy will be reflected in mean scores of 1.0-2.9 on Category I—Who is responsible for policy-making?—while higher, more participatory scores of 3.0-5.0 in the later years would indicate that the specialist elites perceive the policy-making process as becoming less ideological over time. (See Table 2.1.)

The general trend is toward increased specialist elite perceptions of their participatory role in the policy-making

11

Table 2.1.   Elite Perceptions of the Policy-Making Arena, 1952-65

Policy-making is the responsibility of
1.0 Party participation solely
2.0 Party participation primarily
3.0 Joint Party-specialist elite participation
4.0 Specialist participation primarily
5.0 Specialist participation solely[a]

Elites	1952	1953	1955	1957	1959	1961	1963	1965	All Years
Party	1.9	1.9	2.0	1.4	2.9	2.7	1.7	2.3	2.1
Economic	000	2.5	2.3	1.5	3.2	3.0	2.8	3.6	2.5
Legal	000	1.3	2.3	2.9	1.7	4.0	2.5	3.8	2.7
Military	(1.8)[b]	(1.6)	1.6	1.3	000	2.2	3.3	2.7	2.1
Literary	1.8	1.0	1.8	2.9	2.4	2.0	2.5	3.1	2.3
All Elites	1.8	1.6	1.9	2.1	2.5	2.6	2.7	3.2	2.4
Specialists	1.8	1.6	1.9	2.1	2.4	2.8	2.8	3.3	2.4

$F (33,106) = 3.089$, significant at .001

[a] An example of position 5.0, taken from the material used in training the coders: The formation of our military world view has taken place in a creative atmosphere . . . and is the result of the common effort of military theorists and practical military people. Thanks to this, we have developed a body of unified theory on the basis of which a broad state program has been carried out to prepare the country and armed forces for the defense of the Fatherland. [*Kommunist Vooruzhennykh sil,* No. 10 (May 1962), p. 12.]
[b] Data for the military were unavailable for 1952 and 1953. The mean score for all elites was assigned the military for these years and noted within the brackets.

arena.[1] Note, for example, the gradual, rather steady increase in Specialist scores from 1953 onward, culminating in 1965 with an instrumental score of 3.3. While the thrust toward greater specialist elite participation is significant, the trend is uneven for each of the individual elites. A zig-zag course is the characteristic pattern, perhaps best described by the un-Leninist notion of *two steps forward one step back.* For the specialist elites, reversals are typically followed by a resurgence which marks an advance beyond the previous low. This dysrhythmic process is a common phenomenon on all the categories and as will be shown is a function of Party-specialist elite conflict.

By dividing the eight sampled years into two equal periods, 1952-57 and 1959-65, overall participatory trends are more readily illustrated in Table 2.2. With a 47% Specialist increase in 1959-65 over the earlier

[1] The number of paragraphs coded for each elite vary for each year. The N for all elites on all five participatory categories are tallied in Appendix C.

Table 2.2.   Elite Perceptions of the Policy-Making
Arena, 1952-57 to 1959-65

Elites	1952-57	1959-65	% Change Over Time
Party	1.8	2.4	+33%
Economic	1.9	3.3	+74%
Legal	2.4	2.9	+21%
Military	1.6	2.3	+44%
Literary	1.9	2.7	+42%
All Elites	1.9	2.7	+42%
Specialists	1.9	2.8	+47%

period, Question I is affirmatively supported—the perceived boundaries of the political arena are expanding over time. As specialist elite participatory attitudes increase, Party dominance decreases: all the elites recognize greater specialist elite participation, although in 1959-65 the Party at 2.4 defines the parameters of the policy-making arena in more restrictive terms than do the Specialists.

Juxtaposed to the belief category—who *is* described as actually making policy—is its counterpart, a value category on who *should* make policy.

Question 2: Are the Specialist elites "pressing" the Party for greater influence in the policy-making arena?

To show the extent of specialist elite "pressure" on the Party for a larger role in policy-making, three operational prerequisites need be met: (1) Specialist scores on the value category (who should participate?) must increase over time; (2) Specialist scores must be demonstrably higher than Party scores; and (3) Specialist scores on the should category must be appreciably higher, more participatory, than their perceptions of who is actually making policy. When all three conditions are met the specialist elites are said to be "pressing" or "pressuring" the Party for a greater role in the political arena. (See Table 2.3.)

Again the trend is toward stronger specialist elite participatory attitudes. In 1963 and 1965 the Specialists are in the instrumental range, and in 1965 only the Party opts for Party dominance. The general trend for Specialists is continuous and marks a steady increase from 1952 through 1965. Developments over time are more clearly demonstrated by comparing the 1952-57 period with 1959-65, as seen in Table 2.4.

In support of the hypothesis that the specialist elites are "pressing" the Party for greater participation in the policy-making arena, the three requisite conditions are met:

Table 2.3.   Elite Values Toward Participation in the Policy-Making
Arena, 1952-65

Policy-making *should* be the responsibility of
   1.0 Party participation solely
   2.0 Party participation primarily
   3.0 Joint Party-specialist elite participation[a]
   4.0 Specialist participation primarily
   5.0 Specialist participation solely

Elites	1952	1953	1955	1957	1959	1961	1963	1965	All Years
Party	1.9	1.4	1.5	2.1	2.1	2.2	2.0	2.4	1.9
Economic	1.0	1.2	3.0	1.6	2.9	3.4	2.7	3.1	2.2
Legal	1.2	1.4	1.9	2.9	2.7	3.2	3.7	3.3	2.5
Military	(1.3)	(1.3)	1.4	2.8	2.3	2.4	3.2	3.4	2.3
Literary	1.4	1.3	2.9	2.7	2.8	3.0	3.1	3.6	2.6
All Elites	1.3	1.3	2.1	2.5	2.6	2.7	2.9	3.2	2.4
Specialists	1.2	1.3	2.3	2.5	2.7	3.0	3.2	3.4	2.4

$F (38,177) = 7.246$, significant at .001

[a] An example of position 3.0 is contained in a speech by Khrushchev at a meeting of agronomists:

You say "Comrade Khrushchev said thus and so." Am I the highest authority in agricultural science? You are President of the Ukraine Republic Academy of Sciences and I am the Secretary of the Party Central Committee. You must help me in these matters, and not I you. I might be wrong, and if I am, you, as an honest scientist, should say: "Comrade Khrushchev, you do not quite understand the matter." If you explain things to me correctly, I will thank you for it. Let us say I was wrong. But you will say, "Comrade Khrushchev said this and I supported him." What sort of scientist is this comrades? This is toadyism and timeserving. (*Pravda,* December 25, 1961.)

Table 2.4.   Elite Values Toward Policy-Making, 1952-57 to 1959-65

Elites	1952-57	1959-65	% Change Over Time
Party	1.7	2.2	+29%
Economic	1.5	2.9	+93%
Legal	2.0	3.1	+55%
Military	1.7	2.9	+71%
Literary	1.9	3.2	+68%
All Elites	1.8	2.9	+61%
Specialists	1.8	3.1	+72%

(1) Specialist scores increase over time. The instrumental average of 3.1 in 1959-65 marks a 72% increase over 1952-57.

(2) By 1959-65 all the specialist elites opt for a more participatory role in policy-making than the Party deems desirable. In every year from 1955 through 1965, Specialist scores are higher, i.e., more participatory, than are Party scores. Since increased specialist elite participation directly reduces Party dominance, the *apparatchiki,* as expected, claim that specialist elite participation in the later period is greater (2.4) than desirable (2.2).

(3) Specialist scores on who should make policy are appreciably higher in the 1959-65 period than on the question who *is* described as making policy, as we see in Table 2.5.

Table 2.5. Comparison of Specialist Elite Perceptions and Values of the Policy-Making Arena

Is-Should Categories	1959	1961	1963	1965	1959-65
Specialist beliefs (who makes policy?)	2.4	2.8	2.8	3.3	2.8
Specialist values (who should make policy?)	2.7	3.0	3.2	3.4	3.1
% should > is	13%	7%	14%	3%	11%

In sum, on the important question of policy-making, a strong participatory trend is manifested by the specialist elites and recognized by the *apparatchiki.* Not denying the Party's ability to check, at least temporarily, elite participatory attitudes,[2] a distinct feature of the post-Stalin period is this attitudinal development away from strict Party dominance.

II. On Decision-Making

In an ideological political system the Party apparat is seen as dominant in local as well as policy level decisions, reserving for itself the role of final arbiter in disputes over implementation.[3]

---

[2] Note, e.g., the effect of Khrushchev's 1957 victory over Malenkov and Zhukov on the economic and military elites, and the effect of the 1962-63 anti-parasite legislation on the legal elite. The zig-zag course for the individual elites is apparently a result of major policy disputes between the *apparatchiki* and specific elite.

[3] In operational terms policy-making refers to decisions which affect the entire USSR or any one republic, while decision-making refers to decisions affecting a region, territory, city, factory, or farm.

Question 3: Over time do the specialist elites increasingly depict themselves as participants in the local decision-making process? [See Table 2.6]

Table 2.6.   Elite Perceptions of the Decision-Making Arena, 1952-65

Decision-making is the responsibility of
  1.0 Party participation solely
  2.0 Party participation primarily
  3.0 Joint Party-specialist participation
  4.0 Specialist participation primarily
  5.0 Specialist participation solely[a]

Elites	1952	1953	1955	1957	1959	1961	1963	1965	All Years
Party	2.4	2.4	2.6	2.6	3.3	4.0	2.1	3.1	2.8
Economic	000	2.5	3.3	2.8	4.2	3.8	2.5	2.2	3.0
Legal	3.0	000	3.1	2.8	2.5	2.8	2.9	2.5	2.8
Military	(2.5)	(2.6)	2.5	2.9	2.2	2.7	3.3	3.0	2.7
Literary	2.1	2.7	4.1	2.9	4.3	2.7	4.0	3.2	3.2
All Elites	2.5	2.6	3.5	2.8	3.1	3.1	2.9	2.8	2.9
Specialists	2.5	2.6	3.2	2.8	3.3	2.9	3.2	2.7	2.9

$F (35,154) = 1.166$, significant at .001

[a] An example of position 5.0 is:
    Indeed, if the chief means to be used in war is nuclear missiles, this means that we are obliged to construct both the theory of the art of warfare, the operational tactical training of troops and their indoctrinating with regard for the use, above all, of these weapons. This means that each officer, master sargent, sargent, soldier, and sailor must learn to act, to carry out his duties and battle orders, as required by the conditions of nuclear-missile war. (*Krasnaya zvezda*, May 11, 1962.)

The years 1959 and 1961 represent the high tide of decentralization. Participatory *apparatchiki* scores in these years mirror Party efforts to increase production and efficiency through increased local autonomy for the specialist elites. By late 1961, however, the Party line changed as the inevitable consequences—"localism," "family circles," and fraud —threatened economic planning and central Party control.

The third question—a predicted Specialist increase over time—is tenuously supported with an 8% participatory increase in 1959-65 over the earlier period, as shown in Table 2.7. The level of elite participatory attitudes in both periods is high, significantly higher than on the policy-making categories, and seemingly reflects greater tolerance by the *apparatchiki* of specialist elite participation at the local level.

Table 2.7. Elite Perceptions of the Decision-Making
Arena, 1952-57 to 1959-65

Elites	1952-57	1959-65	% Change Over Time
Party	2.5	3.1	+23%
Economic	2.9	3.2	+11%
Legal	2.9	2.6	−12%
Military	2.6	2.8	+ 8%
Literary	3.1	3.6	+18%
All Elites	2.8	2.9	+ 5%
Specialists	2.8	3.0	+ 8%

With an instrumental score of 3.0 in 1959-65, the Specialists perceive themselves as relative equals to the *apparatchiki* in decision-making.

Question 4: Are the Specialists "pressing" the Party for greater influence on the decision-making level. [See Table 2.8.]

Table 2.8. Elite Values Toward Participation in the Decision-Making Arena, 1952-65

Decision-making should be the responsibility of
   1.0 Party participation solely
   2.0 Party participation primarily
   3.0 Joint Party-specialist participation
   4.0 Specialist participation primarily
   5.0 Specialist participation solely[a]

Elites	1952	1953	1955	1957	1959	1961	1963	1965	All Years
Party	3.1	2.8	3.4	2.1	3.7	3.6	2.3	2.1	2.9
Economic	3.3	4.0	4.3	2.2	4.5	3.8	4.0	4.2	3.8
Legal	1.7	3.6	3.3	3.3	4.1	4.1	3.2	3.4	3.4
Military	(2.9)	(3.3)	2.3	4.1	3.0	2.9	2.9	3.2	3.1
Literary	3.8	2.6	3.7	3.2	3.9	4.5	3.2	3.4	3.5
All Elites	2.9	3.0	3.3	3.0	3.9	3.7	3.3	3.3	3.3
Specialists	2.9	3.1	3.3	3.2	3.9	3.8	3.4	3.6	3.4

F (37,194) = 1.767, significant at .001

[a] An example of position 5.0, taken from Khrushchev's speech at the Moscow Writers' Union:
   I do not think I ought to take up an analysis of your works in my address. I am not a literary critic, as you know, and for that reason do not feel called on to analyze your literary works. (*Pravda*, May 22, 1959).

For specialists, instrumental scores on who *should* make decisions are manifested in every year from the death of Stalin onward, and a 16% overall increase is recorded over time, as we see in Table 2.9. In both

Table 2.9. Elite Values Toward Decision-Making 1952-57 to 1959-65

Elites	1952-57	1959-65	% Change Over Time
Party	2.7	2.9	+ 7%
Economic	3.4	4.1	+21%
Legal	3.0	3.7	+23%
Military	3.0	3.0	000%
Literary	3.3	3.6	+ 9%
All Elites	3.1	3.5	+13%
Specialists	3.1	3.6	+16%

periods the Specialists score in the instrumental range, and in 1959-65 all the specialist elites "press" for greater participation than the *apparatchiki* believes desirable.

When specialist elite perceptions of the decision-making process (who makes decisions?) are compared to elite values (who should make decisions?) two patterns emerge, which are evident from table 2.10.

(1) Despite ups and downs through the years, in each of the sampled years the Specialists opt for greater responsibility in local decision-making than they depict themselves as having.

(2) Of all the elites in the 1959-65 period, only the *apparatchiki* claims that elite participation (perceived by the Party to be 3.1) is greater than desirable (2.9). If it is true that the Party apparat is seeking a formula for balancing a high level of specialist elite participation with Party control, a comparison of *apparatchiki* to Specialist scores on the category who should make decisions suggests that the specialist elites seek to upset the mini-max formula at the Party's expense, as found in Table 2.11.

Scanning the data on the decision-making categories it appears that the military is closest to the Party's position, but this compliance is, as will be demonstrated in the discussion of Party-specialist conflict, directly traceable to Zhukov's defeat in 1957, and scores in the later years suggest that the military has strengthened its position since the Cuban missile crisis. The economic elite, despite its decline in 1957 following Malenkov's fall and Khrushchev's industrial reorganization, scores in the instrumental range on decision-making, reflecting a degree of success in its drive for greater managerial influence at the

Table 2.10. Comparison of Specialist Perceptions of the Decision-Making Arena to Specialist Participatory Values, 1952-65

Should-Is Categories	1952	1953	1955	1957	1959	1961	1963	1965	1952-57	1959-65	All Years
Who makes decisions?	2.5	2.6	3.2	2.8	3.3	2.9	3.2	2.7	2.8	3.0	2.9
Should make decisions?	2.9	3.1	3.3	3.2	3.9	3.8	3.4	3.6	3.1	3.6	3.3
% should > is	16%	19%	3%	14%	18%	31%	6%	33%	11%	20%	14%

Table 2.11.   Comparison of Party and Specialist Values Toward
Participation in Decision-Making (Who Should Make Decisions?)

Elites	1952-57	1959-65	All Years
Party	2.7	2.9	2.8
Specialists	3.1	3.6	3.4
% Spec. > Party	15%	24%	21%

factory level. (Scores on the policy level follow a similar course.) The
legal elite—the only specialist elite to perceive a decline in participation on the decisional level, apparently a result of the Party's post-1958
retreat on socialist legality—topped all elites with a 23% increase over
time on who should make decisions, indicating dissatisfaction with
Party dominance. (An identical pattern occurred on the policy-making
categories.) In both the 1952-57 and 1959-65 periods, the literary elite
scored in the participatory range on decision-making and is, predict-
ably, kept from still higher scores by the more Party-oriented attitudes
articulated in the conservative journal *Oktyabr.* All in all, specialist
elite participation in the decision-making arena is appreciable at 2.9 for
All Years, and "pressure" to enhance their participatory role (3.4 for
All Years) is growing increasingly strong over time.

III. Authority Sources in Problem Solving

A relationship exists between the form of political system and the
type of rationalizations used in initiating, defending, and criticizing
policy decisions. Historically, the dominance of the Party apparat in the
Soviet political system is linked to its claim of ideological supremacy.
Certain sources of authority are supportive of *apparatchiki* dominance,
e.g., the justification of policy decisions based on an appeal to Leninist
historical consciousness, whereas other authority sources, for instance,
a policy recommendation based on empirical evidence or specialized
knowledge, are more conducive to specialist elite participation in the
political process. In the category tapping the authority sources appealed to by the five elites in justifying their recommendations on policies and decisions, lower scores of 1.0-2.4 reflect a Party dominant
ideological system, scores in the 2.5-3.5 range are conducive to joint
Party-specialist participation, and the higher scores of 3.6-5.0 support a
still more instrumental environment for specialist elite participation.

*Question 5: Over time, as elite participation increases, do the
elites opt for more instrumental forms of justification?* [See
Table 2.12.]

Table 2.12. **Elite Justifications for Policy Recommendations 1952-65**

What is the authority source appealed to in policy and decision making? How are policy decisions justified?

1.0 Recommendations are based on an understanding of the laws of historical development/by analogy to a theory or decision of Marx, Lenin, Stalin *in the past*

2.0 Recommendation is generally derived from Marxism, Leninism, Stalinism

3.0 Recommendation is derived from Marxism, Leninism, Stalinism, in conjunction with practice/scientific Marxist-Leninist analysis/Marxism and objective analysis[a]

4.0 Recommendation is based on expert opinions/the clash of opinions/discussion

5.0 Recommendation is derived from objective investigation/by empirical methods/by scientific findings

Elites	1952	1953	1955	1957	1959	1961	1963	1965	All Years
Party	2.3	2.5	2.8	3.3	3.9	3.4	3.1	2.5	2.9
Economic	2.1	2.6	3.2	2.8	3.1	3.1	3.8	3.6	3.1
Legal	1.5	2.7	3.2	3.8	3.5	3.7	4.0	3.2	3.1
Military	(2.1)	(2.5)	2.3	2.6	2.3	2.3	2.7	2.9	2.5
Literary	2.2	2.2	2.5	3.4	3.3	2.5	3.2	3.1	2.9
All Elites	2.1	2.5	2.8	3.2	3.4	2.9	3.3	3.1	2.9
Specialists	2.0	2.5	2.8	3.1	3.1	2.9	3.4	3.2	2.9

F (38,209) = 2.661, significant at .001

[a] An example of position 3.0:

Marxism is not an "universal master key" which can be applied without studying practice and without analyzing the data of practice. Authors who construct their conclusions merely on superficial analogies, [position 1.0] or interpretations, comparisons, and "analyses" of quotations [position 2.0] and not on the study of facts—on the study of life—need to be reminded of how the founders of Marxism described the significance of the theory they established. (*Kommunist,* No. 7, 1955).

As specialist elite participatory scores increase it is hypothesized that the elites will tend increasingly to justify and criticize policy decisions in more instrumental terms, since appeals to historical consciousness and ideological awareness are more supportive of *apparatchiki* dominance. Comparing the two periods, the trend over time marks a significant change away from strict ideological appeals. This trend is apparent from Table 2.13.

With Specialists in the instrumental range in four of the last five years and showing a 23% increase over time, the hypothesis is generally affirmed. In the 1959-65 period all elites but the military tend to evalu-

Table 2.13.   Elite Justifications for Policy Recommendations,
1952-57 to 1959-65

Elite	1952-57	1959-65	% Change Over Time
Party	2.8	3.2	+14%
Economic	2.6	3.5	+35%
Legal	2.8	3.5	+25%
Military	2.4	2.6	+ 8%
Literary	2.7	3.0	+11%
All Elites	2.6	3.2	+23%
Specialists	2.6	3.2	+23%

ate policies in instrumental terms more conducive to specialist elite
participation. Party scores are high too; throughout the Khrushchev
years from 1957-63, the Party scored in the instrumental range. This
development may qualify as one indicator of what some observers,
notably Barrington Moore, foresee as a Soviet potential for "technical-
rational" development.[4]

IV. Participatory Attitudes: An Overview

Although the categories are analytically distinct, all relate to the basic
question of elite participation. By collapsing the categories into one
dimension and averaging each elite's score on all five categories, a
Grand Mean score is derived which may serve as a general indicator
of overall participatory trends in the post-Stalin period (Table 2.14).
Readily visible at the outset is the year by year instrumental increase

Table 2.14.   Elite Attitudes Toward Participation: All
Categories Combined 1952-65

Elites	1952	1953	1955	1957	1959	1961	1963	1965	All Years
Party	2.3	2.2	2.5	2.3	3.2	3.2	2.2	2.5	2.6
Economic	2.2	2.6	3.2	2.2	3.6	3.4	3.1	3.3	2.9
Legal	1.9	2.3	2.8	3.2	2.9	3.6	3.3	3.2	2.9
Military	2.1	2.2	2.0	2.7	2.5	2.5	3.1	3.0	2.5
Literary	2.2	2.0	3.0	3.0	3.4	2.9	3.2	3.3	2.9
All Elites	2.1	2.2	2.5	2.7	3.1	3.0	3.0	3.1	2.8
Specialists	2.1	2.2	2.7	2.8	3.1	3.1	3.2	3.2	2.8

[4] *Terror and Progress—USSR* (New York: Harper Torchbooks, 1954), Chap. 7.

for Specialists from 1952 through 1965. Participatory trends are manifested by all the elites, as we see from Table 2.15. A 24% All-Elite

Table 2.15. Elite Attitudes Toward Participation: All
Categories Combined, 1952-57 to 1959-65

Elites	1952-57	1959-65	% Change Over Time
Party	2.3	2.8	+22%
Economic	2.5	3.4	+36%
Legal	2.6	3.2	+23%
Military	2.5	2.7	+ 8%
Literary	2.6	3.2	+23%
All Elites	2.5	3.1	+24%
Specialists	2.6	3.1	+19%

increase in the latter period is significant and indicative of the rapidity of change since Stalin. Through 1959-65, Specialists scores are in the participatory range and in 1963 and 1965 every specialist elite is over 3.0.

The military is perennially low among the specialists and at times below the *apparatchiki* as well. In all probability this reflects Party efforts to exercise exceptionally rigorous political controls over the military. Although not readily apparent from the figures, Marshal Zhukov's removal in 1957 was a crucial development in *apparatchiki*-military relations. By comparing attitudinal scores from an equal sample of articles from the representative military journal, *Krasnaya zvezda*, for the period immediately preceding and following Marshal Zhukov's ouster, the effects of Zhukov's dismissal on the military elite are demonstrated in Table 2.16.

Table 2.16. Military Attitudes Surrounding Marshal Zhukov's Dismissal

Categories	Pre-Zhukov Ouster	Post-Zhukov Ouster	All 1957
Who makes policy?	1.7	1.0	1.3
Who *should* make policy?	3.6	1.5	2.8
Who makes decisions?	3.5	2.0	2.9
Who *should* make decisions?	4.4	2.8	4.1
Authority source	2.7	1.9	2.6
All categories combined	3.3	1.9	2.7

The "price" Khrushchev paid for the military's support against the anti-Party group was for a time exceedingly high. From the data, Zhukov's major thrust was for greater autonomy in the decision-making arena: a score of 4.4 represents a virtual denial of Party influence over local level military affairs. Not until 1963—following the Cuban missile crisis—did the military recover from the post-Zhukov crackdown.[5] The decline in military scores following an open confrontation against the Party is a characteristic pattern for all the specialist elites, again demonstrating the Party's capacity to thwart, temporarily, elite participation in the political process.

While a dysrhythmic pattern of elite attitudinal behavior is typical for all the categories, 1963 marks a crisis year in Party-elite attitudinal relations, for contrary to earlier developments the Party's retreat in 1963 to a more Party dominant position was *not*, as in the past, accompanied by a general decline for the specialist elites but by an overall Specialist increase to a more instrumental position.[6] In short, Party-elite attitudinal relations became significantly more conflicting as both Party and elites denied one another a dominant role in the political arena.

V. Party-Specialist Elite Relations

The *apparatchiki*, confronted with stronger elite participation scores than it considers desirable and with still higher elite aspirations, finds it increasingly difficult to enforce "mini-max" boundaries on the specialist elites. Comparing elite perceptions and values, two types of Party-elite relations may be identified: *accommodation* or *conflict*. Accommodation exists when both the *apparatchiki* and specialist elites substantially agree on the allocation of responsibility in policy and decision making. Conflict—opting for mutually exclusive positions— exists when the Party and elites substantially disagree on the allocation of responsibility in the political arena.[7]

---

[5] Secondary support marking the missile crisis as a turning point in military-Party relations is found in Thomas Wolfe, *Soviet Strategy at the Crossroads* (Cambridge: Harvard University Press, 1964), and Roman Kolkowicz, *The Soviet Military and the Communist Party* (Princeton: Princeton University Press, 1967).

[6] See Carl Linden, *Khrushchev and the Soviet Leadership* (Baltimore: Johns Hopkins University Press, 1966), for a discussion of the Cuban missile crisis as a variable in Khrushchev's fall and as a possible cause for the Party's loss of control over the elites in 1963 and 1965, esp. pp. 146-147.

[7] In operational terms, accommodation exists when the Party's score on the participatory categories is higher than the elite's score, i.e., when the specialist score is within the Party's prescribed boundary of the political arena. (E.g., if the Party score is 2.90 and the specialist score 2.50, the extent of accommodation is —.40, the minus sign denoting accommodation.) Conflict exists when the specialist elite score is more participatory than that of the Party. (E.g., if the Party score is 2.50 and the elite score 3.00, the level of conflict is + .50, plus signs denoting conflict.) For clarity all mean scores are carried two decimal places in the accommodation-conflict tables. A "crisis" is said to exist when the level of Party-specialist conflict is exceedingly high.

Tentatively:

> *Question 6: As specialist elite participation increases, does Party-elite conflict increase?*

And:

> *Question 7: As specialist elite participation increases beyond Party dominance, i.e., beyond mini-max boundaries, does the intensity of conflict increase?*

Focusing on system-wide trends, Party-elite relations may be typed by comparing differential scores on the All Scores Combined Category, as in Table 2.17. All-Year differential scores show that the economic, literary, and legal elites are in attitudinal conflict with the *apparatchiki*. The military, at −.03, is in a "bare bargain" relationship. The years 1952, 1959, and 1961 are periods of accommodation, 1955, 1957, 1963 and 1965 years of conflict. Since 1959 and 1961 are the only two years in which the Party scored in the instrumental range, Party-elite accommodation in these two years is largely due to the Party's permissive definition of the boundaries of the political arena. With a + .27 All-Year conflict score, those years above the mean constitute "crisis years"; rank ordered the crisis years in Party-Specialist relations are 1963, 1965, and 1957, notably, all periods related to succession crises, thereby lending support to the notion that when the central Party is internally divided specialist elite participation increases.

On scanning the differential scores of the individual elites an interesting pattern emerges: following an open confrontation against the Party, the elite typically moves from conflict to accommodation, then, in the next sampled year back into a conflict relationship with the Party. For example, note the "two-steps-forward, one-step-back" pattern for the economic elite in the years from 1955 thru 1959, the legal elite's 1959 accommodating position following the Party's 1958 retreat on the Fundamental Laws, and the military's 1959 score following Marshal Zhukov's ouster. Accommodation, it appears, is *enforced* accommodation—is a result of successful *apparatchiki* efforts to thwart specialist elite encroachments in the political arena, rather than a sign of a consensual definition of the boundaries of the political system. Within this framework, conflict signifies the Party's inability to check the participatory beliefs and aspirations of the specialist elites.

As anticipated in Question 6, Party-elite conflict increases over time, as seen in Table 2.18. A threefold increase in conflict over time is significant, especially so when it is recalled that All-Elite participation scores on the combined category increased by 24%, and the Party

Table 2.17. Party-Elite Relations: Accommodation or Conflict: All Categories Combined, 1952-65*

Elites	1952	1953	1955	1957	1959	1961	1963	1965	All Years
Economic	−.17	+.35	+.73	−.12	+.36	+.23	+.91	+.88	+.37
Legal	−.48	+.07	+.29	+.84	−.30	+.37	+.03	+.78	+.34
Military	−(.20)	+(.05)	−.47	+.44	−.74	−.69	+.80	+.56	−.03
Literary	−.13	−.22	+.49	+.69	+.16	−.25	+.97	+.82	+.36
Specialists	−.24	+.02	+.23	+.45	−.12	−.10	+.95	+.77	+.27

* minus scores denote accommodation, plus scores conflict.

Table 2.18. Party-Elite Relations: Accommodation or Conflict
All Categories Combined, 1952-57 to 1959-65

Elites	1952-57	1959-65
Economic	+.20	+.60
Legal	+.18	+.47
Military	−.05	−.02
Literary	+.21	+.43
Specialists	+.12	+.37

moved from 2.3 in the early period to a "mini-max" score of 2.8 in 1959-65. In the later period, then, Party-elite conflict increases at a sharper rate than does elite perceived participation, thereby supporting the predicted increase in intensity of conflict as Party dominance is threatened by the specialist elites.

Attitudinal conflict characterizes *apparatchiki*-elite relations in the post Stalin period and in particular the later years. This conflict is becoming generalized throughout the system. All the participatory dimensions are in conflict, as we find in Table 2.19. Two inferences may be drawn from this comparison of conflict scores. First, the focus of Party-specialist elite conflict is changing over time: in 1952-57 the question of elite participation on the local decision-making level is most in conflict, while in 1959-65 participation in the policy-making arena ranks as the major source of *apparatchiki*-elite conflict. Since specialist elite participation in the policy-making arena threatens the Party's integrative role, this development may well constitute a most serious challenge to the Party apparat's dominant position in the Soviet political system.

Second, while all dimensions but the perceived boundaries of the decision-making arena are in conflict in 1959-65, this one instance of accommodation is a result of the Party exceeding its "mini-max" boundaries with a co-participatory score of 3.1. That responsibility for decision-making is in contention is apparent from the + .73 1959-65 conflict score on who should participate—the Party opting for 2.9 (the absolute maximum level for maintaining dominance in the decision-making arena), while the Specialists deny Party dominance with a 3.6 average. Thus, by the later period the 2.5-2.9 mini-max range no longer represents the boundaries of compromise but a field of conflict.

VI. Conclusion

Three systemic trends emerge from a review of the data:

(1) Elite participatory attitudes show a marked increase over time, reaching the instrumental level in 1959-1965. By plotting All-Elite

Table 2.19. Party-Specialists Relations: Accommodation or Conflict, 1952-65

Categories	1952	1953	1955	1957	1959	1961	1963	1965	All Years
Who makes policy?	−.14	−.26	−.08	+.71	−.47	+.14	+1.13	+1.05	+.26
Who should make policy?	−.69	−.06	+.82	−.43	+.49	+.75	+1.15	+.93	+.48
Who makes decisions?	+.10	+.23	+.63	+.21	−.01	−1.13	+1.10	−.32	+.10
Who should make decisions?	−.11	+.25	−.17	+1.08	+.15	+.24	+1.02	+1.50	+.50
Authority sources	−.36	−.04	−.04	−.18	−.78	+.50	+.32	+.71	+.02
All categories	−.24	+.02	−.23	+.45	−.12	+.10	+.95	+.77	+.27

Party Dominance   Specialist Participation
(ideological)   (instrumental)

Fig. 2. The Ideological-Instrumental Continuum: All-Elite Scores
on All Participation Categories

grand mean scores on the ideological-instrumental continuum this trend is graphically depicted in Figure 2.

(2) *Attitudinal conflict characterizes apparatchiki-specialist elite relations in the post-Stalin period.* Party-elite conflict on the participatory categories exists in both periods. In 1952-57, with a Specialist participation score of 2.5, the extent of Party-elite conflict is + .12, while in 1959-65 the level of Specialist participation climbs to 3.1 and the level of conflict to + .37. In short, as specialist elite participatory attitudes increased by one-quarter, Party-elite conflict showed a three-fold increase, despite the Party's move from 2.3 to a "mini-max" position of 2.8.

(3) Concomitant with the attitudinal development toward more instrumental elite participatory scores and the intensification of Party-elite conflict is the trend toward an erosion of the ideological foundations of Party dominance—toward what Almond and Powell call the "secularization of values."[8] *Over the years all the elites, the apparatchiki included, increasingly come to rely on scientific knowledge and expert skills as crucial resources in the decision-making process.*

---

[8] Gabriel A. Almond and G. Bingham Powell, Jr., *Comparative Politics: A Developmental Approach* (Boston: Little, Brown & Co., 1967), pp. 24-25; the secularization of culture is described as:

> . . . the process whereby traditional orientations and attitudes give way to more dynamic decision-making processes involving the gathering of information, the evaluation of information, the laying out of alternative courses of action, the selection of a course of action from among these possible courses, and the means whereby one tests whether or not a given course of action is producing the consequences which were intended.

The Party's capacity to dominate what Stalin fondly called the "commanding heights" is an empirical question, not an absolute given in the post-Stalin period. This is not to deny that the *apparatchiki* is more powerful than the specialist elites, but rather that the Party is *not* omnipotent. In the following chapters data are brought to bear on the second operational measure of instrumental systemic trends, namely, the extent to which the specialist elites constitute groups.

PART TWO

The Soviet Elites as Groups

In an ideological political system, societal groups are portrayed as "transmission belts" (Stalin's term) which are denied the wherewithal to articulate or aggregate non-Party interests or develop group consciousness. A key feature of an instrumental system is the existence of interest groups in the political system.[1] Group consciousness, it is reasoned, is in-

---

[1] A concise introduction to the role of pressure groups may be found in Harry Eckstein, "Group Theory and the Comparative Study of Pressure Groups," in Harry Eckstein and David Apter, eds., *Comparative Politics: A Reader* (New York: The Free Press, 1963), pp. 389-397. S. N. Eisenstadt presents a suggestive analysis of the role of skill groups in bureaucratic systems (treating knowledge and skills as political resources) in *The Political Systems of Empires* (New York: The Free Press, 1963). For a general discussion of the role of groups in the Soviet political system see: Michael Gehlen, Group Theory and the Study of Soviet Politics, University of California, Berkeley, monograph; Joel J. Schwartz and William Keech, "Group Influence on the Policy Process in the Soviet Union," *American Political Science Review*, Vol. LXIII, No. 3 (September, 1968), pp. 840-851; H. Gordon Skilling, "Interest Groups and Communist Politics," *World Politics*, Vol. XVIII, No. 3 (April, 1966), pp. 435-451; Donald D. Barry, "The Specialist in Soviet Policy-Making: The Adoption of a Law," *Soviet Studies*, XVI, 2 (October,

herently inimical to Party dominance, for the development of group identity would allow the specialist elites to more readily counter *apparatchiki* priorities and more easily advance coherent alternatives.

Trends toward a more instrumental political system would be reflected in the development of measurable indicators of group consciousness among the specialist elites. Three operational conditions must be present if the elites are to meet the sociological requisites of a group:

First, *group self-consciousness*, the elites must be conscious of themselves as a distinct entity. In the Soviet political context the specialist elites must conceive of themselves as a group distinct from the Party *apparatchiki*.

Second, *ascribed group status*, the elites must be perceived as groups by other elites.

Finally, the elites must possess *a set of shared values* which distinguish them from the other elites, here again particularly from *apparatchiki* values.

In Chapter 3, group self-consciousness and ascribed group status are measured. In Chapters 4-7, elite attitudes toward major political problems of the post-Stalin period are analyzed and an attempt made to determine the extent to which the specialist elites manifest distinct group values.

1964), pp. 152-165; and Frederic J. Fleron, Jr., "The Soviet Political Elite: Aspects of Political and Economic Development in the USSR," Paper presented at the 1968 Annual Meeting of the American Political Science Association, Washington, D.C., September 2-7, 1968. Recent studies which focus on *apparatchiki*-elite group relations include: Jeremy Azrael, *Managerial Power and Soviet Politics*, (Cambridge, Mass.: Harvard University Press, 1966); Priscilla Johnson, *Khrushchev and the Arts: The Politics of Soviet Culture, 1962-1964* (Cambridge, Mass.: M.I.T. Press, 1965); and Roman Kolkowicz, *The Soviet Military and the Communist Party* (Princeton, N.J.: Princeton University Press, 1967).

3 Group Self-Consciousness and Ascribed Group Status

Group self-consciousness and ascribed group status are measured by a special word count category in which all references in the sampled articles which refer to one of the elites by means of a representative *collective noun* are tallied. The representative nouns for each elite are:

The Party Apparat	"Party leaders," "Party officials," "*apparatchiki*," "Party secretaries," "Party spokesman"
The Economic Elite	"economists," "economic planners," "economic administrators," "state administrators"
The Legal Elite	"jurists," "advocates," "legal specialists"
The Military Elite	"military officers," "Marshals," "Generals," "Admirals," "the military"
The Literary Elite	"workers in culture," "writers," "artists," "(literary) editors"

As one indicator of "groupism" (*gruppovshchina*), the collective noun offers a simple and reliable measure of elite group status. By coding all representative plural references (excluding all references to specific people and institutions) the collective noun connotes a perception of group status on the perceived elite by the perceiver. An underlying assumption of this category is that elite group visibility (acknowledgements of one elite by another) is a general approximation of elite prominence; that is, the number of references to one elite by another reflects the saliency of that elite to the perceiver. For example, if the Party refers to the military more often than to any other elite in a given year (as it did in 1957), this is treated as one measure of the importance attributed to the military by the *apparatchiki* in that year. By tallying all references to and by each elite, a measure is derived for inferring the relative prominence of the elites in the political system over time.

It is hypothesized that elite group consciousness increases over time and correlates with increased elite participation. Specifically, the three sociological prerequisites of groupness—group self-consciousness, ascribed group status, and a set of commonly held values—should increase proportionately with elite participation. (See Figure 1.) Before testing a set of hypotheses on the relationship between elite participation and *gruppovshchina*, however, the extent to which the elites meet the definitional conditions of groups must be determined. Table 3.1 contains the data on elite group consciousness.

I. Elite Group Self-Consciousness

Elite group self-consciousness is expected to increase over time. In Table 3.2, the elites are rank-ordered in terms of their number of self references. Expressions of group self-consciousness, virtually nonexistent under Stalin (All-Elites/11), develops rapidly through the years. An 84% increase in 1959-65 over 1952-57 is statistically significant and lends support to the hypothesis that the specialist elites are developing a sense of group identity over time. Advances in group self-consciousness are greatest in the immediate post-Stalin years: an All Elite increase of 191% in 1953 over 1952, a 100% increase in 1955 over 1953, and a 67% increase in 1957 over 1955. In only one year, 1959, is there a decline, this by 39%, followed by gradual increases throughout the later period.

Fluctuations in elite group self-consciousness parallel a general pattern similar to that uncovered on the participatory categories: sharp increases and decreases in the group consciousness of the specialist

Table 3.1. Elite Group References

Elite	1952	1953	1955	1957	1959	1961	1963	1965	All Years
Party									
APPARATCHIKI*	3	10	21	29	15	17	25	23	143
economic	4	6	14	12	10	12	16	19	93
legal	0	3	2	5	9	7	9	10	45
military	1	3	7	15	4	7	15	11	63
literary	0	0	3	13	12	17	18	18	81
all other elites	5	12	26	45	35	43	58	58	282
Total: all elites	8	22	47	74	50	60	83	81	425
Economic Elite									
apparatchiki	2	5	15	12	13	10	14	13	84
ECONOMIC	4	9	17	11	16	18	22	24	121
legal	0	4	4	5	9	10	12	11	55
military	1	1	5	10	6	8	13	12	56
literary	1	2	4	5	5	10	12	11	50
all other elites	4	12	28	32	33	38	51	47	245
Total: all elites	8	21	45	43	49	56	73	71	366
Legal Elite									
apparatchiki	1	3	8	11	12	9	13	9	66
economic	1	4	7	6	8	9	10	13	58
LEGAL	2	6	5	15	13	19	16	20	96
military	1	1	4	2	2	2	6	5	29
literary	1	2	4	7	4	7	10	9	44
all other elites	4	10	23	32	26	27	39	36	187
Total: all elites	6	16	28	47	39	46	55	56	293
Military Elite									
apparatchiki	—	—	9	18	11	8	16	12	74
economic	—	—	8	12	8	9	14	13	64
legal	—	—	0	4	2	5	4	3	18
MILITARY	—	—	8	33	10	13	23	20	107
literary	—	—	3	8	11	10	15	15	62
all other elites	—	—	20	42	34	34	49	43	218
Total: all elites	—	—	28	75	42	45	72	63	325
Literary Elite									
apparatchiki	3	6	10	17	7	11	15	19	88
economic	5	7	9	11	14	14	10	11	81
legal	0	3	1	6	8	8	9	10	45
military	0	1	5	10	5	4	10	7	42
LITERARY	2	7	13	19	23	17	29	31	141
all other elites	8	17	25	44	34	37	44	47	256
Total: all elites	10	27	38	63	57	54	73	78	397
ALL ELITES TOTALS	32	83	186	302	237	261	356	349	1806

* The elite in capital letters is the perceiver; the elites in lower case letters, the perceived.

Table 3.2. Elite Group Self-References

1952	1953	1955	1957	1959	1961	1963	1965	All Years
Eco/4	Pty/10	Pty/21	Mil/33	Lit/23	Leg/19	Lit/29	Lit/31	Pty/143
Pty/3	Eco/9	Eco/17	Pty/29	Eco/16	Eco/18	Pty/25	Eco/24	Lit/141
Leg/2*	Lit/7	Lit/13	Lit/19	Pty/15	Pty/17*	Mil/23	Pty/23	Eco/121
Lit/2*	Leg/6	Mil/8	Leg/15	Leg/13	Lit/17*	Eco/22	Mil/20*	Mil/107
Mil/NA	Mil/NA	Leg/5	Eco/11	Mil/10	Mil/13	Leg/16	Leg/20*	Leg/96
All/11	All/32	All/64	All/107	All/77	All/84	All/115	All/118	All/608

* Score tied.

38

elites reflects the elite's relationship to the Party. Typically, *as elite participatory scores increase, expressions of elite group self-consciousness increase.* And, *following a losing confrontation against the Party, measures of elite group self-consciousness temporarily decline.* This correlation between group consciousness, elite participation, and Party-specialist conflict will be analyzed in the concluding chapter. Let it suffice for the moment to merely illustrate the pattern by tracing the course of the military elite. In 1957 the military ranks first among all elites in expressions of group self-consciousness, recording a four-fold increase over 1955.[1] Following Khrushchev's victory over Marshal Zhukov, the military elite experiences a sharp decline which all but destroys its sense of group identity. As may be recalled from the analysis of elite participatory scores, the military recouped in 1963 following the Cuban missile crisis. This comeback is reflected in the data on military self-consciousness with a 77% increase in 1963 over 1961. Although the military does not match its 1957 level of self-consciousness it does show a significant increase, 61%, in 1959-65 over the early period.

Trends over time reveal that every elite manifests a substantial increase in group self-consciousness, as demonstrated in Table 3.3.

Table 3.3.   Elite Group Self-References, 1952-57 to 1959-65

1952-57	1959-65	All Years	% Change over time*
Party/63	Literary/100	Party/143	+ 27%
Economic/41	Party/80	Literary/141	+144%
Military/41	Economic/80	Economic/121	+ 95%
Literary/41	Legal/68	Military/107	+ 61%
Legal/28	Military/66	Legal/96	+143%
All-Elites/214	All-Elites/394	All-Elites/608	+ 84%

* 1952-57 to 1959-65 changes: $x^2 = p < .05$.

Although the *apparatchiki* ranks as the most self-conscious elite group for All-Years, in the later period the literary elite ranks above the Party, and the economic elite manifests as great a sense of group identity as does the Party. In the 1952-57 period the Party's tally of 63 self-references is 65% higher than the specialist average, whereas in the 1959-65 period the Specialist average is a mere 1% lower in self-consciousness

---

[1] The military elite's tally of 33 references in 1957 is the highest manifested by any elite in any year, thereby lending support—along with the military's high participatory scores just prior to Marshal Zhukov's ouster—to Party criticism of Zhukov for undermining the "leadership and control of the Party." (*Pravda,* November 4, 1957)

than the Party. Thus, over time the Specialists appear to be strengthening their sense of group self-consciousness at a greater rate than the *apparatchiki*.

The most striking changes involve the literary and legal elites, both of which record profound rates of growth over time. Within the literary elite the "liberal" faction, represented by *Novy mir*, manifests the most group self-consciousness (55% of the literary total in 1952-57, 61% in 1959-65), followed by *Oktyabr*, with *Literaturnaya gazeta* a weak third.

By way of summary, the data on elite group self-consciousness support the first definitional condition of *gruppovshchina*—all the specialist elites record a marked increase in self-awareness. If it is valid to assume that expressions of specialist elite group consciousness are inimical to Party dominance, then the trend toward group consciousness manifested by each specialist elite constitutes an indirect diminution of Party dominance, and may be reasonably interpreted as an indicator of systemic change toward a less ideological political system.

II. Ascribed Group Status

Data on the second condition of groupism—ascribed group status—are tabulated in Table 3.4. The elites are rank-ordered according to the number of group references received by each elite from all the other elites. Acknowledgements of the existence of elite groups increase substantially over time. All-Elite tallies show a 108% increase from 1952-57 to 1959-65. As with elite group self-consciousness, the greater increases in ascribed group status occur in the early period, and the only drop in references is a 22% decline in 1959.

The dramatic rise and decline experienced by the military elite lends support to the assumption underlying the category that visibility is a measure of elite prominence. After recording a six-fold increase in visibility from 1953 through 1957, the military suffers a marked decline to last place following Marshal Zhukov's dismissal, a pattern, it will be recalled, duplicated on the participatory categories. This suggests that when Khrushchev was dependent on the military for active support against the economic elite and the so-called "anti-party group" in the Presidium, the military elite developed a strong sense of group self-consciousness (a three-fold increase in 1957 over 1955), and described itself as a co-participant with the Party in the political arena (3.3 on the participatory categories in early 1957). As a consequence, in the eyes of the other elites, the military became the second most prominent elite group in 1957. The sharp decline in visability after 1957 to last place in 1959-61 also parallels the military's experience on the participatory

Table 3.4. Ascribed Group Status

1952	1953	1955	1957	1959	1961	1963	1965	All Years
Eco/10	Eco/17	Pty/42	Pty/58	Pty/32	Eco/44	Pty/58	Eco/56	Pty/312
Pty/6	Pty/14	Eco/38	Mil/43	Eco/40	Lit/44	Lit/55	Pty/53	Eco/296
Mil/3	Leg/10	Mil/21	Eco/41	Lit/34	Pty/38	Eco/50	Lit/53	Lit/237
Lit/2	Mil/6	Lit/14	Lit/33	Leg/28	Leg/30	Mil/44	Mil/35	Mil/190
——	Lit/4	Leg/7	Leg/20	Mil/17	Mil/21	Leg/34	Leg/34	Leg/163
All/21	All/51	All/122	All/195	All/160	All/177	All/241	All/231	All/1198

41

categories, suggesting that until the Cuban missile crisis the *apparat-chiki* had succeeded in reestablishing strict Party controls over the military.[2]

Comparing the 1952-57 to the 1959-65 period, overall trends may be readily discerned from Table 3.5. All the elites show a marked increase

Table 3.5.   Ascribed Group Status, 1952-57 to 1959-65

1952-57	1959-65	All Years	% Change over time*
Party/120	Party/192	Party/312	+ 67%
Economic/106	Economic/190	Economic/296	+ 79%
Legal/37	Legal/126	Legal/163	+ 24%
Military/73	Military/117	Military/190	+ 60%
Literary/52	Literary/184	Literary/237	+240%
All/389	All/809	All/1198	+108%

* 1952-57 to 1959-65 changes: $x^2 = p < .001$.

in ascribed group status, thereby indicating that the second sociological condition of groupism is increasingly being met.

If the number of references to a specific elite is an indicator of the relative prominence of that elite, a comparison of *apparatchiki* to Specialist tallies suggests that over time the Specialists are strengthening their group identity vis-a-vis the Party: in the 1952-57 period the number of elite references to the Party are 79% greater than is the average number of elite references to the Specialists, whereas in the later period this Party-specialist disparity is reduced by one-half. Thus, on this measure of *gruppovshchina*, by 1959-65 the Specialists—particularly the economic and literary elites—constitute a potential challenge to Party dominance in so far as they have established a group identity among the elites which is as salient as that of the *apparatchiki*. Illustrative of this relative strengthening of specialist elite group consciousness is the fact that while the Specialists record a 63% increase in references to the *apparatchiki* over time, they average a 111% increase in self-consciousness, and a 160% average increase in references to the other specialist elites.

[2] Although no category in the study specifically relates to the question of how or why the Party was so successful in subordinating the military (note, e.g., how rapidly the other elites recover following a confrontation with the Party) one possibility—aside from the fact that the military is so organized that control is more easily established—is that the military is at variance with all the other specialist elites on several key values. For example, as will be shown shortly, on the crucial question of resource allocation, the military is at odds with all the elites, and thus is, perhaps, unable to generate much support among the other specialists against Party controls.

In short, although the Party is the most prominent group in both periods, in 1959-65 the specialist elites make appreciable gains in group consciousness and show a significant increase relative to the *apparatchiki*. To the extent that group consciousness is inimical to Party dominance the data suggest that in the later periods the specialist elites have developed a sense of identity which is distinct from that of the *apparatchiki* and thereby constitutes a base from which the specialist elites could better thwart the Party's efforts to arrest the development of non-Party group values and strivings for group autonomy.

The final sociological condition of group consciousness is that the specialist elite hold a set of beliefs and values which differentiate it from other groups, particularly in the Soviet context from the *apparatchiki*. Attitudinal data for each elite are generated through four policy-oriented categories, all of which deal with major problem areas of the Soviet system and relate to the central question of Party dominance. The categories are:

1. On Elite Socialization;
2. On the Role of the Party;
3. On the Allocation of Resources; and
4. On Mobilizing the Population.

Each elite's attitudes on the policy categories are aggregated into an elite orientation—a set of attitudes toward the Party's position in the political system. Two classes of elite orientation may be derived from the data: (1) an ideological orientation is one which tends to support the Party's dominant role in the political system; and (2) an instrumental orientation is one which tends to support specialist elite participation.[3] *To qualify as a strategic elite group, the specialist elite must manifest an instrumental policy orientation.* Further, just as the specialist elites manifested more participatory role perceptions through the years, it is anticipated that the elites will develop an instrumental policy orientation to support their participatory efforts.

Finally, Party-elite attitudinal orientations are expected to be in conflict. By comparing Party to elite orientations it is possible to measure the extent of *apparatchiki*-elite policy conflict in a given year and determine if the level of conflict is increasing over time.

---

[3] See Richard Lowenthal's analysis of ideology as a support of Party dominance in "The Logic of One-Party Rule," *Problems of Communism,* VII, No. 2 (March-April 1958), pp. 21-30. Also, see Frederick C. Barghoorn, "Soviet Political Doctrine and the Problem of Opposition," *Bucknell Review,* XII (May, 1964), pp. 11ff., for a discussion of the linkage between ideological values and Party dominance.

As a framework for interpreting the findings, a general correlation is expected between: (a) specialist elite participation, (b) Party-elite conflict over participation, (c) the development of specialist elite instrumental policy orientations, and (d) Party-elite conflict over policy orientations.

4 On Agents Responsible for Political Socialization

A principle function of political systems is the socialization of citizens into becoming sympathizers and supporters of the system. "At a minimum," Brzezinski and Huntington argue, "political socialization involves the creation of a public interest in: the society or political community as a whole; the political regime or form of government; political groups within the system, such as parties; the ideology and values of the system; and active participation in the political system."[1] Citizens learn, in Verba's phrase, "a patterned set of orientations to politics."[2]

In the Soviet political system the Party apparat attempts to inculate the desired (Party dominant) attitudes and behavior through the *direct* indoctrination of individuals and groups. "The individual is bound to the political system not through primary group loyalties but rather through direct

---

[1] Brzezinski and Huntington, *op. cit.*, p. 77.
[2] Sidney Verba, "Comparative Political Culture," in Lucian W. Pye and Sidney Verba, eds., *Political Culture and Political Development* (Princeton, N. J.: Princeton University Press), p. 165.

subordination of his loyalties to the system."[3] In an ideal-type ideological political system the politization of the citizenry by a single
socialization agent produces a unified political orientation (an ideology) designed to promote active support for the system, e.g.,
"the new Soviet man." While the Soviet Union is not an ideal state,
note, e.g., the "serious deficiencies" uncovered in the *Komsomolskaya
pravda* opinion polls,[4] Brzezinski among others treat the Soviet system
as ideological in that "the Communist Party does attempt to mold all
the political attitudes of the citizens."[5]

In a more participatory, instrumental, political system, responsibility
for political socialization is *dispersed* among various agencies (the family by all accounts being the most influential), and the political orientation is basically *diffuse*—not an overt, systematic, and dogmatic
ideology, but a belief system, a generalized outlook involving "certain
fundamental preferences, prejudices, and often unverified and inartic-
ulated assumptions, without a formal structure and official interpre-
ters."[6] The diffuseness of an instrumental orientation stems in large part
from the absence of a single agent which in an ideological system
dominates the socialization process and denies the development of competitive value orientations.

The dominance of the Party apparat in the Soviet political system is
linked to its ability to impose a Party orientation on the specialist elites.
For the Party, *partiinost* (Party-mindedness) serves to undermine specialist elite group consciousness by placing loyalty to the Party above
elite group values. For the specialist elites *qua* elite groups, the ability
to socialize its members to group norms is a necessary condition for
maintaining a viable position vis-a-vis the *apparatchiki*. This is especially important in the Soviet system where the higher ranking members of the elites are Party members.. If the specialist elites are to
challenge *apparatchiki* dominance in the political arena, it is incumbent
on them to counter the Party's role as the chief agent responsible for
elite socialization and emphasize their own responsibility for the development of group values.[7]

---

[3] Brzezinski and Huntington, *op. cit.*, p. 77.

[4] See *Komsomolskaya pravda*, May 19, 1960, October 7, 1960, January 11, and
January 26, 1961.

[5] Brzezinski and Huntington, op. cit., pp. 77-78; also see Richard C. Gripp's
Patterns of Soviet Politics (Homewood, Illinois: Dorsey Press, 1967), Chap. V, for
a discussion of the Soviet socialization process.

[6] Brzezinski and Huntington, *op. cit.*, p. 23.

[7] The term "elite socialization" refers to that particular socialization process
whereby individuals are socialized into professional occupational roles. See Percy H.
Tannenbaum and Jade M. McLeod, "On the Measurement of Socialization," *Public*

Party dominance would be reflected in specialist elite acknowledgements of the Party and Party organizations as the primary agents responsible for the socialization of the elite. Trends toward a more instrumental political system—one in which the specialist elite groups develop participatory attitudes—would be reflected in an increased emphasis on the elites themselves as the primary agents responsible for the socialization of their members. Because the focus is on Party-elite relations, those paragraphical themes which deal with the family, schools, and mass media in socializing young people are excluded.

Operationally, the ideological positions in the socialization category are: the *Party* and *Party organizations* (e.g., Komsomol, Agitprop, and the Party-State Control Commission). Positions which tend to support the specialist elites are: *occupational groups*[8] (i.e., socialization through membership in the elite, specifically attributed to professional training, peer group influence, or as so frequently cited by the military, the common experiences of World War II), *literature*, and *the courts* (but *not* the Comrade Courts).[9] Table 4.1 shows the basic data on elite perceptions of who is responsible for socialization.

The party

In every year the Party perceives itself as the primary agent responsible for socialization, with "Party organizations" ranking second for All-Years. The role of "occupational groups" is constantly low in both periods, while the influence of "literature" and "the courts" tends to be depreciated over time. When *apparatchiki* perceptions are compared to those of the specialist elites, two diametrically opposed trends are readily visible: (1) in both periods the Party assigns greater weight to its own socialization role than do the specialist elites, and (2) whereas

---

Opinion Quarterly, XXXI, No. 1 (Spring 1967), pp. 27-37, for the distinction between this particular process and the more general socialization process whereby basic values are inculcated in the population. See, too, Jack Dennis, "Major Problems of Political Socialization Research," *Midwest Journal of Political Science*, XII, 1 (February 1968), pp. 85-114.

[8] An example of "occupational group" [the military] as a socializing agent:
> It is necessary for [political officers] to assist them [the commanders], but not by replacing battalion, company, or platoon commanders just because you have presumably more experience. If you interfere with the commander's work, if you go over his head, the result will be destructive and will end in disorder, and where there is disorder, there is conflict, struggle, and catastrophe. (*Krasnaya zvezda*, November 1, 1958)

[9] Comrade Courts were excluded from the category because they are not staffed by professional jurists but by "volunteers." Soviet jurist opposition to the Comrade Courts is discussed by Harold Berman, "The Struggle of Soviet Jurists Against a Return to Stalinist Terror," *Slavic Review*, XXII, No. 2 (June 1963), pp. 319-320.

Table 4.1. Recognized Socialization Agents*

Elites		1952	1953	1955	1957	1959	1961	1963	1965	1952-1957	1959-1965	All Years
PARTY	N=	(23)	(16)	(19)	(16)	(18)	(17)	(21)	(23)	(74)	(79)	(153)
The party		52	69	47	44	46	41	77	47	56.8	54.0	55.4
Party organizations		30	00	11	13	31	18	5	22	12.2	18.5	15.4
Occupational groups		4	6	32	19	7	35	5	17	13.2	12.0	12.6
Literature		9	19	5	13	15	6	10	9	12.2	9.7	11.0
The courts		4	6	5	13	00	00	5	4	5.2	2.7	4.0
ECONOMIC	N=	(8)	(7)	(11)	(6)	(10)	(10)	(14)	(26)	(32)	(60)	(92)
The Party		75	100	27	50	10	20	25	14	62.5	18.5	40.5
Party organizations		00	00	00	00	00	10	15	7	00.0	8.0	4.0
Occupational groups		00	00	36	50	50	40	45	57	22.2	48.0	35.1
Literature		00	00	27	00	20	10	00	14	6.2	10.5	8.4
The courts		25	00	9	00	20	20	15	7	9.0	15.8	12.4
LEGAL	N=	(16)	(21)	(8)	(10)	(13)	(23)	(24)	(25)	(55)	(85)	(140)
The party		94	53	50	40	31	13	25	4	62.2	18.0	40.1
Party organizations		00	00	00	00	00	00	00	4	00.0	.5	.3
Occupational groups		00	4	25	10	15	52	38	52	6.7	39.7	23.2
Literature		00	29	00	00	00	00	00	00	6.7	00.0	3.4
The courts		6	14	25	50	54	34	38	40	24.2	41.2	32.7
MILITARY	N=	(—)	—	(29)	(28)	(33)	(18)	(33)	(33)	(57)	(117)	(174)
The party		—	—	42	54	18	17	6	38	45.5	17.7	31.6
Party organizations		—	—	00	00	12	33	22	3	00.0	17.2	8.6
Occupational groups		—	—	53	43	42	38	58	64	50.5	50.0	50.3
Literature		—	—	4	4	18	6	10	3	3.0	10.0	6.5
The courts		—	—	00	00	9	6	3	3	00.0	5.5	2.8

Table 4.1.—Continued

Elites		1952	1953	1955	1957	1959	1961	1963	1965	1952-1957	1959-1965	All Years
LITERARY	$N=$	(19)	(23)	(43)	(16)	(30)	(18)	(26)	(33)	(101)	(107)	(208)
The party		37	26	12	6	10	18	23	9	20.0	15.0	17.5
Party organizations		5	00	23	13	00	6	4	3	10.0	3.7	6.9
Occupational groups		5	22	7	6	17	18	23	21	9.3	18.7	14.1
Literature		53	43	51	57	63	51	49	61	51.5	56.5	54.0
The courts		00	9	7	19	10	6	00	15	8.7	5.2	7.5
TOTAL	$N=$	(66)	(67)	(110)	(76)	(95)	(85)	(118)	(140)	(319)	(448)	(767)

* level of significance of chi squares:

1952-57	1959-65	Over Time
Pty × Eco: p not sig.	Pty × Eco: $p < .001$	Pty : p not sig.
Pty × Lit : $p < .01$	Pty × Leg: $p < .001$	Eco: $p < .001$
Pty × Mil : $p < .001$	Pty × Mil : $p < .001$	Leg: $p < .001$
Pty × Lit : $p < .001$	Pty × Mil : $p < .001$	Mil : $p < .001$
		Lit : p not sig.

the Party increasingly emphasizes its role through the years, the specialist elites unanimously tend to depreciate the Party's role over time. Both patterns are demonstrated in Table 4.2.

Table 4.2.   Elite Perceptions of the Influence of the Party and Party
Organizations as Socializing Agents Over Time

Elites	1952-57	1959-65	% Point of Change Over Time
Party	69%	73%	+ 4
Economic	63%	29%	−34
Legal	62%	19%	−43
Military	46%	35%	−11
Literary	30%	19%	−11
Specialists	50%	25%	−25

All the specialist elites tend to deemphasize the Party's role. For Specialists the perceived influence of the "Party" and "party organizations" declines by 50% over time. Thus, the changing elite perspectives suggest that the *apparatchiki* plays a less influential role over time in the direct socialization of specialist elite members. On the surface—and further study need be done—the Party, represented by the two central Party *apparat* journals, perceives itself as the dominant agent responsible for developing *apparatchiki* group values, while each of the specialist elites increasingly frees itself from Party influence.

The economic elite

Over time the economic elite undergoes a dramatic shift away from acknowledgements of the Party's responsibility for elite socialization. In the early period "the Party" is cited as the primary agent responsible for elite socialization, accounting for approximately two-thirds of the economic elite's perceptions. In 1952-57 the role of the economic elite in the socialization process (best approximated by the tally on "occupational groups") is weak, 22%, and the role of "literature" and "the courts" is minimal. In only one year in the early period (1955, when you will recall, the elite's participatory scores reached the instrumental range) does the economic elite succeed in subordinating the role of the Party. By contrast, in the 1959-65 period the economic elite succeeds in reducing the role of "the Party" to manageable proportions, 21%, and establishes the responsibility of "occupational groups" as the primary source of group norms. Both "literature" and "the courts" are also given a more substantial role, accounting for one quarter of the elite's

1959-65 total. Thus, throughout 1959-65 the economic elite is apparently free of the pervasive influence of the Party in the socialization of its members.

The legal elite

Following the Specialist trend illustrated in Table 4.2, the legal elite tends to depreciate the role of "the Party" over time—from 62% in 1952-57 to 18% in 1959-65. In this later period both "the courts" and "occupational groups" rank above "the Party" in importance to the legal elite.

For the legal elite both "the courts" and "occupational groups" are equally favored throughout the later period and are apparently interchangeable as suitable socialization agents. The legal elite's most frequently cited source of group values—professional training and peer group influence—are perceived as being influential in both "the courts" and "occupational groups." That the courts could represent a Party rather than a legal elite agent is not supported in the data; note, e.g., the Party's rejection of "the courts" in both periods, 5% in 1952-57 and 3% in 1959-65. Quite possibly the courts, especially comrades' courts, are perceived as socializing agents for inculcating values for the general population, but it appears that the courts are not channels for Party socialization of the legal elite. This interpretation—differentiating between the role the court plays vis-a-vis the population and its role in developing legal elite group norms—may explain the rather low value assigned it by the other specialist elites. As an agent of socialization the courts apparently have but a minimal influence on the values of the other elites.

The military elite

In both periods the military cites the role of "occupational groups" as the primary agent responsible for elite socialization, the influence of "the Party" as secondary. Over time the military's commitment to "occupational groups" is relatively constant, 50% for All-Years, with the major change through the years being the depreciation of the role of "the Party" from 46% in the early period to 18% in the later.

The question of who is responsible for the socialization of elite group values appears to be related directly to the issue of elite autonomy. The data suggest that following Zhukov's ouster, Party-military conflict increased in two stages: from 1959-61 the military depreciated the role of "the Party," and from 1963-65 more heavily weighted the role of the military in the socialization process. It would appear, therefore, and this is supported in Roman Kolkowicz's recent study of Party-military relations,[10] that throughout the later period the military elite moved to free itself from Party controls over group values.

The literary elite

The Specialist trends outlined in Table 4.2 are supported by the literary elite: the role of "the Party" is depreciated over time, and those agents more conducive to the development of intra-elite values are given primacy. The literary places less emphasis on "occupational groups" than do the other specialist elites, but perceives "literature" as the primary socializing agency, 52% in 1952-57, 57% in 1959-65.

Whereas the legal elite treats "occupational groups" and "the courts" as relatively equal and acceptable agents, the literary elite ranks "literature" first, "occupation groups" a distant second, but nonetheless higher than "the Party" in 1959-65. This may well reflect the fact that the literary function is more a solitary than a collective effort, hence group values are not derived through literary groups, e.g., writers' unions, but through literature itself. Then too, because of the liberal-conservative factionalism within the literary elite there is no single intra-elite agent which serves to reinforce and modify values.

Based on the factional differences exhibited within the literary elite on all the categories, it appears that each of the factions looks to a small number of literary sources for support and reinforcement. The result is the often voted "we"-"they" distinction between conservatives and liberal writers. Addressing the Eighth Plenum of the Russian Writers' Union, one writer noted that "the basis [for literary criticism nowadays] is not *what* is printed, or *how* it is written, but where it is printed. If it is in *Oktyabr* then they [the liberals] would say "let's go after it." [11]

Factional differences on this category are particularly pronounced. For All-Years *Oktyabr* perceives "the Party" as influential for 34% of its total, *Literaturnaya gazeta* 54%, and *Novy mir* 12%. Since the literary elite's All-Year score for "the Party" is but 18%, the data suggest that neither the conservative nor liberal faction greatly favors Party intervention in elite group affairs. If Priscilla Johnson's argument is correct, namely, that the Party plays off one faction against the other,[12]

---

[10] *Op. cit.*, Chap. 5.
[11] Semion Tregub, *Literaturnaya Rossiia*, No. 15 (April 12, 1963), p. 1.
[12] Priscilla Johnson, *Khrushchev and the Arts: The Politics of Soviet Culture, 1962-1964* (Cambridge, Mass.: M.I.T. Press, 1965), pp. 1-89.

it appears that both contending factions fear direct Party intervention more than officially tolerated intra-elite strife.

The specialist elites

The anticipated increase in instrumental values over time is strongly supported in the data. As was shown in Table 4.2, each of the specialist elites perceives a decline in the influence of "the Party" and "Party organizations" over time, and in the later period ranks "occupational groups," "literature," or "the courts" above "the Party" as primary socialization agents.

To test the predicted increase in Party-elite conflict over time, the Party's commitment to elite socialization is compared in Table 4.3 to the specialist's perception of the Party's role. Conflict exists when the Party's role is depreciated by the specialist elite, accommodation when the specialist elite accepts the Party's perception of its role.

Each specialist elite manifests a significant increase in conflict with the *apparatchiki* over time, with the Specialists recording a four-fold increase in 1959-65 over the early period. Years of Party-Specialist "crisis," i.e., those years when the level of conflict is above the All-Year average, are 1959, 1963, and 1965. Each of these years are also "crisis years" on the participatory category Who Should Make Decisions, suggesting that as the specialist elites pressed for a greater role in the decision-making arena they also moved to depreciate Party influence in the elite socialization process.

Table 4.3. Party-Elite Conflict/Accommodation on Who Is Responsible for Socialization*

Elites	1952	1953	1955	1957	1959	1961	1963	1965	1952-1957	1959-1965	All Years
Economic	+ 7	−31	+31	+ 7	+67	+29	+42	+48	+ 4	+47	+26
Legal	−12	+16	+ 8	+17	+46	+46	+57	+61	+ 7	+53	+30
Military	—	—	+16	+ 3	+47	+ 9	+54	+38	+10	+37	+28
Literary	+40	+43	+23	+38	+67	+35	+55	+59	+36	+54	+45
Specialists	+12	+ 9	+20	+16	+57	+30	+52	+52	+10	+48	+29

* Plus signs denote the extent of conflict, minus scores the extent of accommodation

5 The Role of the Party

In the Soviet historical context, the linkage between the supremacy of the *apparatchiki* and the Party's commitment to ideological goals tends to support Party dominance by denying the specialist elites a sanctioned basis for a non-Party identity and a rationale for "loyal opposition." Data on elite attitudes toward the Party's role are generated through two interdependent categories—one tapping elite perceptions, the other elite values:

1. Elite perceptions of what is the party's present role
2. Elite values on what the party's role should be

An ideological orientation toward the Party's role—one which supports *apparatchiki* dominance—would be reflected by such justifications as the Party's *historical consciousness,* its efforts on behalf of *socialist democracy,* and the *building of communism.* Conversely, trends toward a more instrumental political system would be reflected in elite attitudes that tend to promote specialist elite participation by placing a premium to those systemic values which require specialist elite cooperation to be achieved. The instrumental values

Table 5.1. Elite Perceptions of the Party's Present Role*

Elites		1952	1953	1955	1957	1959	1961	1963	1965	1952-1957	1959-1965	All Years
PARTY	$N=$	(20)	(22)	(23)	(33)	(36)	(18)	(40)	(44)	(98)	(138)	(236)
Collective wisdom/ understand history		5	27	4	10	00	31	25	31	10.7	21.7	16.2
Social democracy/ classless society		35	18	4	10	30	16	13	9	17.2	16.1	17.1
Economic achievements/ growth		15	22	28	36	36	27	13	21	25.2	24.0	24.6
Scientific/technological advance		20	10	8	30	27	16	25	18	17.2	22.0	19.6
Living standard		5	5	25	10	3	11	15	18	10.7	11.7	11.2
Defense of the USSR		20	18	32	3	3	5	10	00	17.7	5.3	11.5
ECONOMIC	$N=$	(21)	(28)	(27)	(47)	(32)	(16)	(20)	(25)	(122)	(93)	(215)
Collective wisdom		00	16	00	2	15	00	00	00	4.7	3.7	4.1
Social democracy		57	10	4	16	9	9	25	4	20.5	13.0	16.7
Econ. achievement		9	16	19	22	6	6	25	32	15.5	16.0	15.8
Sci. advancement		24	22	44	19	49	61	00	12	27.5	30.7	29.2
Living standard		5	26	28	36	15	24	20	44	25.0	25.7	25.4
Defense of the USSR		5	10	4	4	6	00	30	8	5.7	10.7	8.1
LEGAL	$N=$	(11)	(15)	(13)	(14)	(14)	(19)	(17)	(63)	(53)	(66)	(119)
Collective wisdom		00	39	35	21	43	20	30	13	23.0	26.5	24.8
Social democracy		72	14	35	51	28	55	46	25	45.2	39.0	42.1
Econ. achievement		00	20	8	00	00	5	00	25	6.2	6.8	6.6
Sci. advancement		9	7	8	7	14	5	00	19	7.2	8.7	8.1

Table 5.1. (Continued)

Elites	1952	1953	1955	1957	1959	1961	1963	1965	1952-1957	1959-1965	All Years
Living standard	9	7	8	21	14	11	24	19	11.0	17.5	14.0
Defense of the USSR	9	14	8	00	00	5	00	00	8.0	1.0	4.4
MILITARY $N=$	(—)	(—)	(27)	(26)	(10)	(32)	(27)	(29)	(53)	(98)	(151)
Collective wisdom	—	—	4	12	00	00	00	7	7.5	2.0	4.4
Social democracy	—	—	28	8	00	22	11	34	16.5	16.5	16.5
Econ. achievement	—	—	12	16	30	3	21	00	15.0	14.2	14.7
Sci. achievement	—	—	16	20	30	31	24	00	19.0	20.2	19.6
Living standard	—	—	4	00	00	3	00	00	1.5	.7	1.1
Defense of the USSR	—	—	36	44	40	40	44	58	40.5	46.2	43.3
LITERARY $N=$	(13)	(13)	(15)	(17)	(27)	(10)	(22)	(29)	(58)	(88)	(146)
Collective wisdom	8	15	13	6	4	20	18	00	11.2	11.5	11.4
Social democracy	24	15	7	18	40	20	9	20	14.5	22.2	18.6
Econ. achievement	36	22	32	40	11	30	27	27	34.5	23.5	29.4
Sci. advancement	8	15	20	18	40	10	00	20	18.0	18.0	18.0
Living standard	8	8	7	12	4	10	27	32	8.2	17.5	12.9
Defense of the USSR	16	22	20	6	00	10	18	00	13.2	6.7	9.8
TOTAL $N=$	(65)	(78)	(105)	(136)	(119)	(95)	(126)	(145)	(384)	(483)	(867)

* level of significance of chi squares:

1952-57
Pty × Eco: $p < .01$
Pty × Leg: $p < .001$
Pty × Mil: $p < .05$
Pty × Lit : p not sig.

1959-65
Pty × Eco: $p < .001$
Pty × Leg: $p < .001$
Pty × Mil: $p < .001$
Pty × Lit : p not sig.

Over Time
Pty : $p < .02$
Eco: p not sig.
Leg: p not sig.
Mil: p not sig.
Lit : p not sig.

tapped in the categories on the role of the Party are: *economic achievement, scientific/technological advancement,* and *improvements in the
standard of living.*[1] One final option—*defense of the USSR*—is included
for its relevance to the question of Party dominance vis-a-vis the military. The data are presented in Table 5.1.

I. The Party's Present Role

The question of the Party's present role is the most salient issue facing the elites on the policy-oriented categories. If it is valid to view
saliency as an indicator of the importance attributed to an issue by the
elites, then it would appear that the Party's present role in the system
(with an All-Elite, All-Year *N* of 867) is the singlemost important question facing the elites.[2] It also appears from the increases in saliency
over time—the Specialists record a 31% increase, the *apparatchiki* a
40% increase—that widespread interest in the Party's role among the
elites is increasing over time, perhaps indirectly reflecting a challenge
to the Party's historical prerogatives of rule. Two additional saliency
trends lend support to this interpretation: first, scanning the All-Elite
totals, the Party's role is most salient in the years 1957, 1963, and 1965—
notably, all years of Party-elite participatory conflict; and second, in
only two years, 1959 and 1961, is there a decline in saliency, both years
when the Party scored in the instrumental range on the participatory
categories. Subject to verification in the ensuing analysis, it is suggested
that the Party's present role is a, if not *the*, major issue of contention
between the Party and specialist elites.

The party

In every year but 1953 the Party stressed its instrumental over ideological roles. Although one-third of the Party's role perceptions are
ideological (i.e., justifications based on "historical consciousness" and socialist democracy"), in both the 1952-57 and 1959-65 periods the Party's
role perceptions are more instrumental (primarily in terms of "economic achievement" and "scientific advance") than ideological.

[1] An example of "standard of living" as a justification of the Party's role is: "The
maximum satisfaction of the material and spiritual needs of our people is the chief
concern of our Party." (From *Pravda,* quoted in *CDSP,* XVIII, No. 7, p. 14.

[2] Compared to the other categories we find that the question of the Party's present
role is 29% more salient than the issue of resource allocation, 24% more salient than
the problem of socialization, and 3% more salient than the question of how to mobilize the population. When both the belief and value categories on the Party's role
are combined, the problem accounts for 47% of the total for all issue-oriented
categories.

The Party's concept of its roles is neither instrumental nor ideological per se, but a mix. In 1959-65 the Party perceives its role in terms of promoting economic and scientific progress, ranking "historical consciousness," its major ideological support, third, and its commitment to "socialist democracy" fourth. As shown in Table 5.2, the end-result is a balance between ideological and instrumental role perceptions.

Table 5.2. The Party's Dominant Role Perceptions*

1952-57		1959-65		All Years	
econ. achieve.	25%	econ. achieve.	24%	econ. achieve.	29%
defense of USSR	18%	sci. advance.	22%	sci. achieve.	20%
soc. democracy	18%	hist. conscious.	22%	soc. democracy	17%
% of Total	61%		68%		66%

* An elite's dominant role perceptions are operationally defined as those options, rank ordered, which account for more than a majority (60%) of the elite's total percentage.

The economic elite

The economic elite's perceptions of the Party's role differ from those of the *apparatchiki* in two key respects: first, in both the 1952-57 and 1959-65 periods the economic elite virtually denies "historical consciousness" as a legitimate justification of the Party's role, and second, tends to depreciate "socialist democracy" as a premise for Party rule.

Increasingly the economic elite ascribes a more instrumental than ideological role to the Party, as shown in Table 5.3. In the later period

Table 5.3. The Economic Elite's Dominant Perceptions of the Party's Role

1952-57		1959-65		All Years	
sci. advance.	28%	sci. advance.	31%	sci. advance.	29%
living standard	25%	living standard	26%	living standard	25%
soc. democracy	20%	econ. achieve.	16%	soc. democracy	17%
% of Total	73%		73%		71%

the economic elite's dominant orientation is totally instrumental. Where the *apparatchiki* and economic elite differ is on question of improvements in the "standard of living"—the economic elite ranking it second for All-Years, the Party relegating it to fifth place. In both periods the economic elite emphasizes the Party's instrumental roles. Of all the specialist elites the economic elite is most committed to an instrumental interpretation of the Party's roles.

The legal elite

Unlike the other specialist elites, the legal perceives the Party's role primarily in ideological terms. In both periods the legal elite's orientation is ideological, principally in terms of "socialist democracy."

If it is true that a specialist elite's failure to ascribe non-ideological roles to the Party fosters an *apparatchiki* dominant relationship between that elite and the Party, the legal elite's failure to attribute a set of instrumental roles to the Party may in part account for the legal elite's weak demonstration of group self-consciousness. Any such interpretation must be tempered, however, by the legal elite's strong showing on the other issue categories which demonstrate that it *aspires* to a more instrumental orientation, just as it aspires to a more participatory role in policy and decision-making.

The military elite

Virtually singleminded in claiming that the Party's primary role is "defense of the USSR," the military elite's perceptions are not shared by the *apparatchiki* or by the specialist elites, all of whom rank "defense" low, the *apparatchiki,* for example, ranking it last in 1959-65. In only one year, 1955, does the Party conceive of its role in terms favorable to the military. Perhaps as a direct consequence of the Party's failure to emphasize "defense," the military leads all the specialists elites in expressing concern (high saliency) over the Party's role in the later period.

As will be more fully analyzed in the ensuing discussion, the military's orientation entails a coherent set of attitudes which set it apart from both the *apparatchiki* and the other specialist elites. Basically, the military consistently favors whatever supports defense spending and opposes whatever competes with their demands on the ruble. Witness, e.g., the military's rejection of "standard of living" as a Party role, and its support for "scientific advancement," "economic achievement," and "socialist democracy." This last position correlates with the military elite's disapproval of all options in all categories which tend to increase non-military spending. Comparing those positions which the military consistently favors with those it opposes, for the military elite "socialist democracy" denotes a system in which consumption is suppressed in favor of capitalization—an interpretation which is more akin to Stalin's usage than to that held by the other elites in the post-Stalin system.

As will become clearer in the ensuing analysis, the military elite is attitudinally isolated from both the *apparatchiki* and the other specialist elites. The end result of this isolation is a double-edged failure: an inability to maintain Party support for its priorities, and—unlike the other specialist elites—an inability to generate an attitudinal orientation which consistently undermines Party dominance.

The literary elite

Despite an increase in references to "socialist democracy" over time, the literary elite perceives the Party's role as being primarily instrumental. More striking than the literary elite's emphasis on the Party's instrumental roles is the factional (conservative, centrist, liberal) variation shown in Table 5.4 within the literary elite.

Table 5.4.   Literary Elite Perceptions of the Party's Ideological Roles: Contribution of Each Faction to Literary Totals

	1952-57	1959-65	All Years
Oktyabr			
historical consciousness	77%	75%	76%
socialist democracy	29%	50%	39%
average	53%	63%	57%
Literaturnaya gazeta			
historical consciousness	22%	25%	24%
socialist democracy	28%	45%	42%
average	30%	35%	33%
Novy mir			
historical consciousness	00%	00%	00%
socialist democracy	33%	5%	19%
average	17%	3%	10%
Literary Elite Total	100%	100%	100%

Oktyabr accounts for over one-half of the literary elite's All-Year ideological total, *Literaturnaya gazeta* for one-third, and *Novy mir* for a mere 10%. Equally important is the total omission of "historical consciousness" as an option by *Novy mir*. On the instrumental side, the major intra-elite differences are reflected on the question of improvements in the "standard of living": *Novy mir* accounts for 54% of the literary elite's total, *Literaturnaya gazeta* and *Oktyabr* for 20% and 26% respectively. What is clear, then, are the profound differences within the literary elite, with the often-cited distinction between the conservatives, middle of the roaders, and liberals supported on this category.

Table 5.5. Elite Values on What the Party's Role Should Be*

Elites	1952	1953	1955	1957	1959	1961	1963	1965	1952-1957	1959-1965	All Years
PARTY $N=$	(13)	(16)	(14)	(21)	(28)	(27)	(35)	(26)	(64)	(116)	(180)
Collective wisdom	8	31	21	14	00	4	18	8	15.7	7.5	11.6
Socialist democracy	8	6	00	00	11	4	9	00	3.2	6.0	4.0
Communism	15	00	00	14	18	30	30	30	6.1	26.7	16.4
World Socialism	00	00	21	5	11	7	12	00	7.1	7.2	7.1
Econ. achievement	38	12	14	19	21	13	9	19	24.0	15.8	19.0
Sci. advancement	23	24	00	19	32	19	3	11	18.3	16.7	17.5
Living standard	00	6	21	19	7	19	6	19	13.8	13.5	13.7
Defense of USSR	8	19	21	10	00	4	12	11	14.8	7.0	10.0
ECONOMIC $N=$	(6)	(38)	(34)	(10)	(14)	(17)	(8)	(5)	(88)	(44)	(132)
Collective wisdom	00	00	00	10	00	00	00	00	1.6	0.0	.8
Socialist democracy	17	00	00	00	2	6	00	00	2.5	1.3	2.1
Communism	00	16	00	00	7	18	13	00	4.2	11.0	7.8
World Socialism	00	13	12	10	00	00	00	00	9.3	0.0	4.7
Econ. achievement	33	32	3	10	14	6	25	20	16.7	15.1	15.9
Sci. advancement	17	13	38	30	11	18	13	40	25.9	21.3	23.6
Living standard	17	26	38	40	64	52	50	40	33.6	50.1	41.9
Defense of USSR	17	00	9	00	00	00	00	00	6.0	0.0	3.0
LEGAL $N=$	(4)	(22)	(9)	(14)	(18)	(17)	(10)	(11)	(49)	(56)	(105)
Collective wisdom	00	45	11	14	6	00	00	00	15.5	1.6	8.6
Socialist democracy	25	00	00	21	22	18	10	00	11.3	12.8	12.1
Communism	25	00	00	00	22	18	30	9	6.3	18.1	12.2
World Socialism	00	00	00	00	00	00	00	00	00.0	00.0	00.0
Econ. achievement	25	9	33	14	6	18	00	18	20.7	11.4	15.1
Sci. advancement	25	9	33	36	39	24	10	36	26.8	28.2	27.5

Living standard	00	36	22	14	6	24	30	36	19.4	24.6	22.9
Defense of USSR	00	00	00	00	00	00	10	00	00.0	2.8	1.4
MILITARY $N=$	(—)	(—)	(17)	(16)	(8)	(37)	(20)	(20)	(33)	(85)	(118)
Collective wisdom	—	—	00	00	00	00	00	5	00.0	1.3	.7
Socialist democracy	—	—	00	00	00	3	15	00	00.0	3.8	1.9
Communism	—	—	00	00	00	22	5	00	00.0	7.2	3.6
World Socialism	—	—	6	00	37	25	00	5	4.2	16.8	10.5
Econ. achievement	—	—	58	31	13	25	15	10	43.0	15.9	29.5
Sci. advancement	—	—	18	31	00	11	45	20	26.9	19.0	22.5
Living standard	—	—	00	00	00	3	5	00	00.0	1.4	.7
Defense of USSR	—	—	18	37	50	11	15	60	26.5	32.9	29.7
LITERARY $N=$	(16)	(25)	(17)	(3)	(13)	(13)	(11)	(6)	(61)	(43)	(104)
Collective wisdom	13	16	6	00	00	8	18	00	7.2	6.9	7.1
Socialist democracy	00	8	00	00	8	15	00	00	1.9	4.7	3.3
Communism	6	16	12	33	22	8	00	17	14.0	10.6	12.3
World Socialism	00	4	00	00	00	15	00	00	1.3	4.2	2.8
Econ. achievement	19	20	18	33	22	15	00	00	23.2	10.0	16.6
Sci. advancement	13	12	12	00	16	8	27	33	9.2	18.1	13.8
Living standard	13	24	53	33	31	23	27	33	26.1	34.2	30.2
Defense of USSR	37	00	00	00	00	8	27	17	16.9	10.6	13.7
TOTAL $N=$	(39)	(101)	(91)	(64)	(81)	(111)	(84)	(68)	(295)	(344)	(639)

* level of significance of chi squares:

1952-57	1959-65	Over Time
Pty × Eco: $p < .001$	Pty × Eco: $p < .001$	Pty : $p < .05$
Pty × Leg: $p < .01$	Pty × Leg: $p < .01$	Eco: p not sig.
Pty × Mil: $p < .01$	Pty × Mil: $p < .001$	Leg: $p < .05$
Pty × Lit : $p < .05$	Pty × Lit : $p < .05$	Mil : p not sig.
		Lit : $p < .05$

The specialist elites

As a collective entity the Specialists show a slight trend toward a more instrumental orientation. What is clear from the data is the Specialists' emphasis on the Party's instrumental roles—in 1952-57 instrumental roles are stressed 33% more than ideological, and in 1959-65 the Specialists' place 47% greater emphasis on the Party's instrumental roles.

II. What the Role of the Party Should Be

Whereas the specialist elites tend to perceive the Party's role as a mixture of ideological and instrumental roles, on the value category (What Should Be the Role of the Party?) all the specialist elites favor the Party's instrumental over ideological roles, and all show a strong tendency to depreciate the Party's ideological roles. Table 5.5 presents the data on elite values toward the Party's role.

The party

While the Party perceived its roles as a blend of ideological and instrumental roles, on the "should" category the *apparatchiki* places somewhat greater value on its ideological roles over time and emphasizes its instrumental roles less. The Party shows a 47% increase in ideological values and an 18% decline in instrumental values over time. With a 40% All-Year commitment to its ideological roles, the *apparatchiki* ranks as the most ideologically oriented elite. The Party's instrumental emphasis, although averaging 50% for All-Years, is well below the Specialist average of 64%.

The Party's dominant value orientation (i.e., those positions which account for over 60% of the elite's total) is weighted in favor of "scientific advance" and "economic achievement." Table 5.6 shows that within the Party's dominant value orientation the emphasis is more on instrumental than ideological roles. Particularly noteworthy is the decline over time of references to "historical consciousness" and the minor value placed on the sacrosanct "classless society" and "world socialism." The Party's primary ideological value is "building communism"—an ill-defined value which ranks as the Party's primary value following passage of the 1961 Party program. This de-emphasis of the traditional mainstays of Party dominance and the stress on "building communism" may more accurately reflect a trend toward the seculari-

Table 5.6.   The Party's Dominant Value Orientation Toward What
Its Role Should Be

1952-57		1959-65		All Years	
econ. achieve.	24%	communism	28%	econ. achieve.	19%
sci. advance.	18%	sci. advance.	17%	sci. advance.	18%
hist. con-		econ. achieve.	16%	communism	17%
sciousness	16%			living standard	14%
defense of USSR	15%				
% of Total	73%		61%		68%

zation of ideological values than a pillar of support for *apparatchiki* dominance.[3]

The economic elite

Of all the elites, the economic elite manifests the least support for the Party's ideological goals and places the greatest value on instrumental roles. The economic elite ranks as the most instrumentally oriented elite in both periods, and its dominant value system reflects this commitment, as seen in Table 5.7. "Economic achievement," another instru-

Table 5.7.   The Economic Elite's Dominant Value Orientation
Toward What the Party's Role Should Be

1952-57		1959-65		All Years	
living standard	34%	living standard	50%	living standard	42%
sci. advance	26%	sci. advance	21%	sci. advance	24%
% of Total	60%		71%		66%

mental role, ranks third in both periods—17% in 1952-57, 15% in 1959-65, thereby strengthening the economic elite's instrumental orientation still more.

When the economic elite's perceptions of the Party's role are compared to its responses on what the Party's role should be, the trend is clearly toward an instrumental orientation. For example, whereas the Party's efforts on behalf of "socialist democracy" were perceived by the

---

[3] As Herbert Ritvo demonstrated in his analysis of the New Party Program, *The New Soviet Society* (New York: The New Leader, 1962), passim, the document is primarily a long-range economic plan. As such, "building communism" entails advances in the economic, scientific, and welfare realms and is thereby dependent on specialist elite contributions.

economic elite as one of the Party's major roles, 17% for All-Years, it is denied as a legitimate value, 3% for 1952-57, 1% in 1959-65. "Historical consciousness" and "world socialism" are rejected by the economic elite as well.

The legal elite

Although the legal elite perceived the Party's role in ideological terms, primarily in terms of "socialist democracy," its value orientation is decidedly instrumental. This value orientation represents a total turnabout for the legal elite, again indirectly supporting the notion that the jurists aspire to challenge *apparatchiki* controls but are unable to effectively counter Party dominance.

Table 5.8 shows that the legal elite's dominant values are weighted

Table 5.8.   The Legal Elite's Dominant Values Toward
What the Party's Role Should Be

1952-57		1959-65		All Years	
sci. advance.	27%	sci. advance.	28%	sci. advance.	28%
econ. achieve.	21%	living standard	25%	living standard	23%
living standard	19%	communism	18%	econ. achieve.	15%
% of Total	67%		71%		66%

in favor of the Party's instrumental roles. Recalling that the legal elite's primary perception of the Party's role was "socialist democracy" (42% All-Years), note that as a value this option now ranks low, 12% for All-Years. The same pattern holds for "historical consciousness," perceived to be 25% All-Years, but as a value it declines from 16% in the early period to 8% in the later. While all the specialist elites manifest a marked tension between what is and what should be, the legal elite suffers the most profound disparity between beliefs and values. This dissonance is perhaps due to the legal elite's inability to break *apparatchiki* dominance over the legal system.

The military elite

The military's primary value favors defense spending, as we see from Table 5.9. The decline in instrumental values is primarily a result of a readjustment in favor of "defense of the USSR" and "world socialism."

The military's emphasis on "world socialism" (4% in 1952-57, 17% in 1959-65, 11% All-Years) is somewhat problematical. While admittedly an ideological value, it does not fit with the military's general orienta-

Table 5.9. The Military Elite's Dominant Values Toward
What the Party's Role Should Be

1952-57		1959-65		All Years	
econ. achieve.	43%	defense of USSR	33%	defense of USSR	30%
sci. advance.	27%	sci. achieve.	19%	econ. achieve.	30%
		world socialism	17%		
% of Total	70%		69%		60%

tion. First, the military elite tends to depreciate the other major ideological supports of Party dominance—"historical consciousness," "classless society," and "communism." Second, whereas the military perceived "socialist democracy" as an important Party role, 17% All-Years, it records little favor for it on the value category, 2% All-Years. In short, except for "world socialism" the military depreciates the Party's ideological goals. Further, the military is the only elite to place any value on "world socialism." Given the military's commitment to a strong economic base for defense, it appears that "world socialism" may well denote a more defensive than revolutionary value, specifically defense of the socialist bloc. If so, and a random check of the sampled paragraphs shows that this value most frequently appears in articles stressing the need for "defense against imperialism," the military apparently values this Party role as a support for greater defense spending.

The literary elite

The literary shows a marked preference for the Party's instrumental over ideological roles. As was true for the literary's perceptual orientation, its dominant values are instrumental, as shown in Table 5.10.

Table 5.10. The Literary Elite's Dominant Values Toward
What the Party's Role Should Be

1952-57		1959-65		All Years	
living standard	26%	living standard	34%	living standard	30%
econ. achieve.	23%	sci. advance.	18%	econ. achieve.	17%
defense of USSR	17%	communism/		sci. advance.	14%
		defense*	11%		
% of Total	66%		63%		61%

* score tied at 11% each.

The literary elite is closest in orientation to the economic elite with its emphasis on the Party's instrumental roles.

Literary intra-elite factional differences are pronounced: *Oktyabr* accounts for the bulk of the literary elite's total ideological score, followed by *Literaturnaya gazeta,* and *Novy mir* last. The increase in ideological values for *Novy mir* are primarily due to references to "communism," not "historical consciousness" or the "classless society," as shown in Table 5.11.

Table 5.11. The Literary Elite's Values Toward the Party's Ideological Roles: Contribution of Each Faction to the Literary's Ideological Total

Factions	1952-57	1959-65	All Years
Oktyabr	72%	50%	61%
Literaturnaya gazeta	23%	23%	23%
Novy mir	5%	27%	16%
Literary total	100%	100%	100%

On the instrumental side, sharp factional differences occur over the question of improvements in the "living standard." *Novy mir* accounts for half of the literary elite's emphasis on improvements in the "living standard," *Oktyabr* for one-third.

In comparing factional perceptions to values, the most radical change is in the devaluation of "socialist democracy" as a legitimate Party goal. Whereas the literary elite perceived this as the second most important Party role, for All-Years 19%, it ranks next to last as a value, 3% All-Years, with *Oktyabr* accounting for two-thirds of this 3% elite total. What is clear, then, is the sharp factional boundaries within the literary elite. In particular, *Oktyabr* and *Novy mir* manifest a distinct set of beliefs and values toward the Party's role.

The specialist elites

Two system-wide trends emerge from a comparison of the Specialists' ideological and instrumental values toward the Party's roles. (1) Each of the specialist elites places greater value on the Party's instrumental than ideological roles. The Specialists' values are seen in Table 5.12. (2) The Party, with a 40% All-Year average on its ideological roles, ranks as the most ideologically oriented elite, 17 percentage points higher than the Specialists, and the Party's 51% emphasis on instrumental roles is 13 percentage points below the Specialists' All-Year average.

Table 5.12. Specialist Values Toward the Party's
Ideological and Instrumental Roles

Specialist Values	1952-57	1959-65	All Years
Ideo. Values	20%	25%	23%
Instru. Values	68%	62%	64%
% Instru. > Ideo.	+48	+37	+41

When Specialist perceptions of the Party's role are compared to
their values on what the Party's role should be, it is clear that the Specialists favor the Party's more instrumental roles, as we see in Table
5.13. In both periods the Specialists invest less value in the Party's ideo-

Table 5.13. Comparison of Specialist Elite Perceptions
and Values of the Party's Roles

Specialists	1952-57	1959-65	All Years
Ideological Perceptions	36%	34%	35%
Ideological Values	20%	25%	23%
% Ideo. Values < Ideo. Perceptions	-16	- 9	-12
Instrumental Perceptions	47%	50%	49%
Instrumental Values	68%	62%	64%
% Instru. Values > Instru. Perceptions	+21	+12	+15

logical roles than they perceive the Party as pursuing, and place greater
value on the Party's instrumental roles than they perceive the Party as
favoring. There is, in short, a sharp disparity between Party and Specialist beliefs and values: the Party believes its ideological and instrumental roles should be balanced, the Specialists that the Party's efforts
should be channeled along instrumental lines.

The Specialist's emphasis on instrumental values is further illustrated
in their dominant value orientation (Table 5.14). In both periods the
Specialists' dominant value orientation is instrumental. ("Defense of
the USSR" ranks fourth in 1952-57 with 6% of the total, and in 1959-65
is tied with "building communism" at 12%.)

The predicted increase in specialist elite instrumental values over
time is supported for each of the specialist elites. The Specialists generally perceive the Party as pursuing both ideological and instrumental
goals, but consistently favor the Party's instrumental roles. Equally
indicative of the Specialists' instrumental orientation is their rejection

Table 5.14.   The Specialists' Dominant Values Toward
What the Party's Role Should Be

1952-57		1959-65		All Years	
econ. achieve.	30%	living standard	27%	econ. achieve.	22%
sci. advance.	22%	sci. advance.	22%	sci. advance.	22%
living standard	16%	econ. achieve.	13%	living standard	22%
% of Total	68%		62%		66%

of those ideological values which most support *apparatchiki* dominance —"historical consciousness," "socialist democracy," and "world socialism" account for but 5% of the Specialists' All-Year average.

The anticipated increase in *apparatchiki*-elite attitudinal conflict over the Party's role may be tested by comparing Party to elite scores on each position. Operationally, conflict exists when the Party's ideological percentages are higher than those of the specialists elite, accommodation when the Party's scores are more instrumental than those of the specialists.[4] In Table 5.15, plus scores denote conflict, minus scores accommodation.

Focusing on the trend for Specialists over time, the early period is characterized by accommodation, a general agreement between the *apparatchiki* and elites on how the Party defines its roles, the later period is one of conflict. The military, economic, and literary elites are, respectively, in a state of conflict with the *apparatchiki*. The legal elite stands with the Party in interpreting the Party's role primarily in ideological terms.

More impressive is the sharp increase in Party-elite conflict over what the Party's role *should* be, as shown in Table 5.16. All the specialist elites are in conflict with the *apparatchiki* on what the Party's role should be. There is a 25% increase in attitudinal conflict over time, and Party-specialist conflict exists in every year following Stalin's death.

When specialist elite perceptions of the Party's role are compared to their value orientation, the instrumental trend is pronounced: all the specialist elites disfavor the Party's ideological roles and come to favor increasingly a stronger instrumental commitment. Judging from the

---

[4] To measure more realistically Party-military conflict and accommodation, both elites' scores on the question of the Party's role in "defense of the USSR" are also calculated. Party-military conflict exists when, in addition to the above condition, the Party's tally on "defense" is less than the military's perception or value. Accommodation exists when the Party's emphasis or commitment to defense is equal to or greater than the military's.

Table 5.15. Party-Elite Perceptions of the Party's Role: Conflict or Accommodation

Elites	1952	1953	1955	1957	1959	1961	1963	1965	1952-1957	1959-1965	All Years
Economic	−21	+46	+34	+ 3	+10	+73	+ 5	+67	+16	+39	+27
Legal	−54	−11	−99	−100	−79	−61	−67	+ 8	−66	−50	−58
Military	−	+23	−23	+ 1	+65	+43	+53	000	−12	+40	+23
Literary	+20	+23	−14	− 10	−25	−11	+12	+41	+ 5	+ 4	+ 5
Specialists	−18	+19	−26	− 27	− 7	+11	+ 1	+29	−14	+ 8	− 1

71

Table 5.16.   Party-Elite Values Toward What the Party's Role Should Be: Conflict or Accommodation

Elites	1952	1953	1955	1957	1959	1961	1963	1965	1952-1957	1959-1965	All Years
Economic	+20	+37	+69	+36	+60	+46	+115	+89	+41	+78	+59
Legal	−30	+ 4	+84	+ 5	−19	+27	+ 51	+68	+13	+32	+24
Military	—	—	+74	+65	+ 6	− 9	+ 89	+58	+70	+36	+47
Literary	− 4	+15	+72	+ 9	+19	+10	+ 77	+38	+23	+36	+30
Specialists	− 5	+19	+75	+29	+17	+19	+ 83	+63	+37	+46	+40

increase in *apparatchiki*-specialist conflict over time, it would appear that the Party's effort to strike a balance between its ideological and instrumental roles no longer (since 1959) satisfies any of the specialist elites, all of whom express opposition to the Party's traditional ideological roles.

6   Resource Allocation

In an ideal-type Party-dominant Soviet political system, the Party apparat monopolizes the resource allocation process. Party campaigns to "storm" one or another problem through an increased outlay of capital, material, or manpower would be trumpeted by the specialist elites. A characteristic feature of a Party dominant system is, then, basic agreement between the *apparatchiki* and elites on the allocation of resources. Trends toward a more instrumental, less Party dominant, political system would be reflected in a growing disagreement between the *apparatchiki* and specialist elites on who gets what, when, how. In a participatory system the specialist elites would tend to press increasingly for expenditures which support their functional interests (e.g., the military favoring a higher military budget) and which deny the *apparatchiki* monopolistic control over the setting of goals and implementation of priorities.

The allocation of resources is an integral function of all political systems and played a critical role in the Party-elite controversies of the post-Stalin period. Under Stalin, given the level of economic development and the political leadership's commitment to rapid industrial growth, economic orthodoxy entailed a highly structured set of priorities geared to promote autarchy —"socialism in one country"—a self-sufficient economic base and a strong military establishment. Synoptically, capital for investment in heavy industry and the military was generated by suppressing consumption—"primitive socialist accumulation," to borrow Preobrazhenski's phrase—specifically, minimum capital investment in agriculture, light industry, and the standard of living.

In the post-Stalin period, with the socialist base built, the question of economic priorities was once again injected directly into the political struggle. To cite the most dramatic example, in Khrushchev's rise to power in 1955-57, the question of resource allocation was a crucial factor in the political conflict between the *apparatchiki*, the economic elite, and the military.

In the category on resource allocation the options are: *the military, heavy industry, light industry, education, improvements in the standard of living,* (e.g., welfare, consumer goods, housing) and *agriculture.*[1] By comparing each elite's responses on the category, it is possible to determine the dominant set of resource priorities for each elite in a given year and over time. Comparing *apparatchiki* to specialist elite priorities a measure is derived for determining the extent of Party-elite accommodation or conflict. Party dominance would be reflected by inter-elite consensus on the allocation of resources, a more instrumental political system by *apparatchiki*-elite dissensus. The data on the allocation of resources appear in Table 6.1.

The party

The apparatchiki—committed to the traditional priorities of "heavy industry" and "military spending" in the early period—undergoes a conspicuous shift over time. The trend away from what are conventionally viewed as the Party's primary values toward a more instrumental set of priorities is significant, and is the most profound shift experienced by any elite on the category, as can be seen in Table 6.2.

This trend reflects a growing concern with the consumer. Note, e.g., that the decline in commitment to "heavy industry" and "the military" directly accounts for the increases in "agriculture," "light industry," and "living standard," all instrumental priorities in that they reflect an effort

---

[1] An example of "improvements in the standard of living" is: "The 1965 plan lays special stress on the expansion of the output of consumer goods and a rise in their quality. The output of consumer articles will be increased by 7.7 percent." (From *Pravda,* quoted in *CDSP,* XVII. No. 7, p. 12.)

Table 6.1. Elite Values Toward the Allocation of Resources*

Elites		1952	1953	1955	1957	1959	1961	1963	1965	1952-1957	1959-1965	All Years
PARTY	$N=$	(10)	(10)	(21)	(25)	(22)	(16)	(21)	(24)	(66)	(83)	(149)
The military		20	30	40	8	00	13	10	4	24.8	7.2	16.0
Heavy industry		40	30	25	32	23	19	14	13	34.5	16.8	25.7
Light industry		10	10	5	4	14	25	14	21	5.7	17.7	11.7
Education		10	10	20	28	18	13	38	21	16.8	22.2	19.5
Living standard		10	10	5	12	5	19	5	21	9.0	13.0	11.0
Agriculture		10	10	5	16	41	13	19	21	9.7	23.0	16.1
ECONOMIC	$N=$	(16)	(19)	(33)	(10)	(33)	(25)	(31)	(24)	(78)	(113)	(191)
The military		19	00	00	10	00	00	00	00	7.0	00.0	3.7
Heavy industry		32	21	25	40	12	16	13	17	29.5	13.5	21.5
Light industry		6	21	31	10	37	32	13	21	16.5	25.7	21.1
Education		12	16	00	00	3	12	13	17	6.8	14.7	10.7
Living standard		6	16	12	00	25	12	16	21	7.5	18.0	12.8
Agriculture		25	27	31	40	25	28	45	25	32.5	30.0	31.3
LEGAL	$N=$	(10)	(16)	(7)	(1)	(2)	(9)	(1)	(10)	(34)	(22)	(56)
The military		10	00	00	00	00	00	00	00	2.0	00.0	1.0
Heavy industry		20	6	00	00	50	00	00	00	7.5	12.5	10.0
Light industry		00	6	00	00	50	00	00	10	1.5	15.0	8.2
Education		40	13	00	100	00	44	00	10	39.5	12.3	25.8
Living standard		10	6	57	00	00	00	00	30	17.5	7.7	12.6
Agriculture		20	69	43	00	00	56	100	50	32.5	52.0	42.3

Table 6.1.—Continued

Elites		1952	1953	1955	1957	1959	1961	1963	1965	1952-1957	1959-1965	All Years
MILITARY	$N=$	(10)	(—)	(20)	(18)	(6)	(9)	(28)	(21)	(38)	(64)	(102)
The military		00	—	55	94	100	67	68	62	73.5	75.2	74.4
Heavy industry		30	—	45	6	00	33	18	00	26.5	12.5	19.5
Light industry		10	—	00	00	00	00	00	00	00.0	00.0	00.0
Education		30	—	00	00	00	00	00	9	00.0	2.0	1.0
Living standard		10	—	00	00	00	00	7	19	00.0	6.3	3.2
Agriculture		30	—	00	00	00	00	7	9	00.0	4.0	2.0
LITERARY	$N=$	(10)	(17)	(13)	(14)	(17)	(7)	(16)	(22)	(54)	(62)	(116)
The military		00	00	00	00	00	00	00	00	00.0	0.0	0.0
Heavy industry		30	17	15	28	12	00	6	00	22.5	4.0	13.3
Light industry		10	6	8	14	24	28	6	18	8.7	20.5	14.7
Education		30	6	31	7	24	28	25	18	15.7	24.2	20.0
Living standard		10	17	00	7	12	00	25	32	8.0	18.0	13.0
Agriculture		30	53	46	43	30	43	38	32	45.3	33.0	39.2
TOTAL	$N=$	(46)	(62)	(94)	(68)	(80)	(66)	(97)	(101)	(270)	(344)	(614)

* level of significance of chi squares:

1952-57	1959-65	Over Time
Pty × Eco: $p < .001$	Pty × Eco: $p < .05$	Pty : $p < .001$
Pty × Leg: $p < .001$	Pty × Leg: p not sig.	Eco: $p < .01$
Pty × Mil: $p < .001$	Pty × Mil: $p < .001$	Leg: p not sig.
Pty × Lit : $p < .001$	Pty × Lit : p not sig.	Mil: p not sig.
		Lit : $p < .05$

Table 6.2.   The Party's Dominant Resource Allocation Priorities

1952-57		1959-65		All Years	
heavy industry	35%	agriculture	23%	heavy industry	26%
the military	25%	education	22%	education	20%
		light industry	18%	agriculture	16%
% of Total	60%		63%		62%

to motivate the population through incentives rather than coercion. Second, and this will be discussed later, the Party's shift in priorities *follows* the orientation of the economic, literary, and legal elites rather than initiating the change. The three specialist elites all manifested these values earlier and with more emphasis than did the *apparatchiki*. While it is impossible to demonstrate a causal relationship, i.e., we are unable to prove that the specialist elites "pressured" the *apparatchiki* to change, the sequence is strikingly illustrated when Party priorities are compared to those of the economic elite. The economic elite's instrumental priorities of 1953-1957, rejected by the *apparatchiki* in the early period, are coopted in the later period. That the Party's shift over time reflects political as well as economic factors is suggested by the Party's sharp de-emphasis of military spending after the Party's victory over the economic elite freed Khrushchev from his dependency on military support.

The economic elite

On this essentially political question of resource allocation, the economic elite leads all elites in saliency, with the Party ranking second— 16% lower than the economic elite in 1952-57, 36% lower in 1959-65. Table 6.3 shows that over time, the economic elite develops a strong set of instrumental priorities.

Table 6.3.   The Economic Elite's Dominant Resource Allocation Priorities

1952-57		1959-65		All Years	
agriculture	33%	agriculture	30%	agriculture	31%
heavy industry	30%	light industry	26%	heavy industry	22%
		living standard	18%	light industry	21%
% of Total	63%		73%		74%

When the Party's orientation is compared to that of the economic elite, it is readily apparent that the economic elite is appreciably more consumer oriented; in 1959-65, e.g., the economic elite favors agricultural investments 7 percentage points more than does the *apparatchiki*, light industry by 8 points, and living standard by 5 points. On the traditional side, the economic elite totally rejects an increase in military spending and, like the Party, assigns a minimal percentage to investment in heavy industry. Thus, despite the Party's significant change over time, the economic elite (as well as the literary and legal elites) manifests a still more instrumental set of priorities than the *apparatchiki*.

The legal elite

Due to the inexplicably low saliency for the legal elite on the question of resource allocation, its yearly totals are not statistically reliable, although it is possible, with obvious reservations, to compare the legal elite's priorities over time[2] (Table 6.4). The legal elite's instrumental

Table 6.4. The Legal Elite's Dominant Resource Allocation Priorities

1952-57		1959-65		All Years	
education	40%	agriculture	52%	agriculture	42%
agriculture	33%	light industry	15%	education	26%
% of Total	73%		67%		68%

commitment is dominant and stronger still when it is noted that "living standard" ranks third, with 13% for All-Years. As is the case with the economic and literary elite, a commitment to agricultural spending is the key priority which separates the legal elite from the *apparatchiki*.

The military elite

The military's orientation is simple, consistent, and forthright—resources should be allocated to "the military," to a lesser extent into "heavy industry," and virtually nowhere else. In every year the military elite's dominant orientation is for military spending, in the early period accounting for 74% of its total, in the later 75%. Not until 1963-65 does the military acknowledge the agricultural crisis, this with a mere 8% in the two years for an All-Year average of 2%. Efforts to raise the "living standard" fare little better, with a 3% average for All-Years.

---

[2] "Inexplicable" for two reasons: (1) in 1952-1953, and to a lesser extent in 1961-1965, the legal elite does discuss the problem; and (2) the literary elite—to cite the most functionally analogous elite vis-a-vis the budgetary process—records a keen interest in the question of resource allocation.

As was suggested in the analysis of the military's perceptions and values of the Party's role, the military elite is singleminded in its pursuit of the ruble. Judging from the Party's 1959-65 priorities on resource allocation, the competition for scarce resources is intensifying over time and all elites but the military show a marked tendency to depreciate military spending as the demands on resources increase. The military stands alone in its commitment to what was once a most privileged sector of the economy.

The literary elite

Over time the literary elite articulates a firm commitment to instrumental priorities, as is apparent from Table 6.5. This instrumental

Table 6.5.   The Literary Elite's Dominant Resource Allocation Priorities

1952-57		1959-65		All Years	
agriculture	45%	agriculture	33%	agriculture	39%
heavy industry	23%	education	24%	education	20%
		light industry	21%	light industry	15%
% of Total	68%		78%		74%

orientation is all the more pronounced in that in 1959-65 "living standard" ranks fourth at 18%, thereby leaving a mere 4% for "heavy industry" and zero for "military spending."

Factional differences within the literary elite on the question of resource allocation are not as pronounced as on the categories tapping elite attitudes toward the Party's role. In the early period *Oktyabr* does tend to support "heavy industry" and *Novy mir* "light industry," but in the later period all three factions share a primary concern with "agriculture" and a uniform de-emphasis of "heavy industry."

The party and the specialists

On the question of resource allocation three elite groupings, rather than the Party-Specialist dichotomy, is discernible. (1) The military elite's orientation is a flat denial of the All-Elite trend toward a more instrumental set of resource priorities. (2) The economic, legal, and literary elites share a primary commitment to agricultural investment and a general consumer orientation. This consumerism is best illustrated by a rank ordering of this grouping's priorities over time. (See Table 6.6.) For All-Years the three specialist elites manifest a dominant orientation toward instrumental priorities. If "living standard" and

Table 6.6. The Economic, Legal, and Literary Elite's Priorities
On the Allocation of Resources

1952-57		1959-65		All Years	
Dominant Priorities					
agriculture	37%	agriculture	38%	agriculture	38%
education	21%	light industry	21%	education	18%
heavy industry	20%	education	17%	light industry	16%
Secondary Priorities					
living standard	11%	living standard	15%	heavy industry	14%
light industry	9%	heavy industry	10%	living standard	13%
military	3%	military	00%	military	2%
Total	101%		101%		101%

"light industry" are collapsed into one position, the strength of the commitment toward consumerism is still more pronounced.

(3) The primary difference between the *apparatchiki* and specialist elite grouping is one of relative emphasis: despite the Party's growing commitment to the consumer, the Party strikes a balance between traditional priorities and what some (Mao Tse-tung, for one) would call a "revisionist" orientation. For all years, e.g., 42% of the Party's priorities are devoted to "heavy industry" and "the military," while the three specialist elites average but 17%. Over time the one priority which best differentiates the *apparatchiki*-specialist grouping is "agriculture," which the economic, legal, and literary elites consistently rank as the primary priority, 22 percentage points higher than the Party for All-Years. The anticipated specialist-elite increase in instrumental values over time is therefore valid for the economic, and legal, and literary elites (and for the *apparatchiki* as well) but invalid for the military elite.

The predicted increase in Party-elite conflict is valid only for the military elite. For the economic, legal, and literary elite, conflict with the *apparatchiki* on the question of resource allocation *declines* over time. Because the *apparatchiki* has undergone such a profound change in its orientation, to gain a meaningful measure of Party-elite conflict the Party's *dominant* value orientation is compared to the *dominant* orientation of the specialist elites. Since some difference is bound to exist between the *apparatchiki* and elites in any but an ideal-type Party dominant system, the question is how much difference constitutes conflict? The standard set here is to use the specialist elite's All-Year average difference with the Party as a base to measure the extent of

Table 6.7. Party-Elite Conflict/Accommodation on the Allocation of Resources

Elites	1952	1953	1955	1957	1959	1961	1963	1965	1952-1959	1959-1965	All Years
Economic	−25	+19	+43	+ 9	+ 1	−17	+14	−41	+46	−43	+ 3
Legal	−47	+ 6	+48	− 1	− 3	+32	+26	−58	+ 6	− 3	+ 3
Military	—	—	−73	+31	+56	+ 5	+ 4	−24	−42	+41	− 1
Literary	−10	+26	+42	− 9	−20	+46	−20	−35	+49	−29	+20
Specialists	−27	+17	+15	+ 8	+ 9	+17	+ 6	−40	+13	− 8	+ 5

accommodation or conflict. Conflict is said to exist when the difference between the Party and elite's dominant values is greater than the elite's All-Year Average. Accommodation exists when the level of Party-elite difference is less than the elite's All-Year average. Table 6.7 shows the Party-Elite conflict scores; plus signs denote the extent of conflict (i.e., the percentage points above the average), minus signs the extent of accommodation.

The economic, legal, and literary elites move from conflict in the early period to accommodation in the later period. For the three elites, the shift from +34 in 1952-57 to −25 in 1959-65 is statistically significant and reflects a basic agreement between the three elites and the *apparatchiki* on the Party's shift toward a more instrumental orientation through the years. The military elite alone records an increase in conflict. As the Party moved toward a more consumer oriented set of priorities, the military maintained its commitment to its traditional interests in heavy industrial and military spending.

All told, it appears that the Party's shift in the 1959-65 period is primarily an adjustment, a redress of the Stalinist priorities, not the abandonment of its commitment to rapid industrialization. Quite obviously the Party's aim is for a more balanced course of development. The economic and literary elite appear to support the Party's new orientation; the legal elite stresses (perhaps correctly) the need for a near-total effort to improve the agricultural sector, while the military resists the Party's new orientation in favor of the traditional priorities.

7 On Mobilizing the Population

A problem of the post-Stalin period—common to all political systems but largely muted during Stalin's time—is the question of how best to motivate the population to fulfill elite systemic goals. Following Stalin's death the issue came to the fore as it became generally accepted among the elites that the economy was in crisis: the agricultural problem, low labor productivity, bureaucratic drag, and a system-wide lack of initiative and efficiency were bemoaned. The ensuing debate, confined within the parameters of the one-party socialist context, may be analyzed along the ideological-instrumental continuum. At the "leftist" pole of the ideological continuum were those who argued for the maintenance of the Stalinist priority in heavy industry and its correlate, the suppression of mass consumption. From this posture the threat of coercion was implied and such ideological incentives as *communist ideals,* the *exemplary behavior of the Party, opposition to bourgeois influences,* and *Soviet patriotism* were stressed as means for motivating the population toward greater productivity. At the other end of the continuum were those instrumental arguments which

84

emphasized *material incentives* and related efforts to gain *popular support*.[1]

In the Party dominant Soviet political system the specialist elites would share the Party's values on how best to mobilize the population. One measure of trends toward a more participatory system would be the extent to which the *apparatchiki* fails to enforce its values on how best to mobilize the population on the specialist elites. Whatever the Party's choice of means, unanimity is judged to be a sign of Party dominance, attitudinal diversity an indicator of a less ideological political system. Further, it is expected that over time the specialist elites will tend to favor "material incentives" and efforts to gain "popular support" over ideological incentives in motivating the population. Underlying this assumption is the belief that a link exists between Party-elite and Party-society relations. More specifically, it is reasoned that it is impossible for the specialist elites to carve out a relatively secure sphere for autonomous action and participation as long as the *apparatchiki* enforces strong ideological demands on the population. Party dominance, the ban on factions and elite participation, is premised on a state of conflict between the political and social system. The alleviation of this antagonism, accomplished partly through instrumental incentives, works to the advantage of the specialist elites in their efforts to break *apparatchiki* dominance in the policy and decision making arenas. Table 7.1 contains the data on elite values on motivating the population.

With an All-Elite total *n* of 841 paragraphs for All-Years, this category ranks as the second most important issue facing the elites, a mere 4% less salient than the category on the Party's present role. For each of the elites the question of how best to motivate the population becomes increasingly important through the years, a 40% increase for All-Elites over time. While the *apparatchiki* deals with the issue most for All-Years, the military elite ranks first in 1959-65 and, since there are no data available for the military for 1952 and 1953, in all probability the military is the elite most concerned with the question for All-Years.

The party

Over time, the apparatchiki demonstrates a marked shift toward more instrumental incentives. Each of the ideological values—"commu-

---

[1] An example of "material incentives" is found in Khrushchev's speech to agricultural workers in Kalinovka: "The scientists and engineers who make rockets are paid well by the state. If they were not paid [well], obviously the development of science and technology would be slowed down." (*Pravda*, August 3, 1963.)

Table 7.1. Elite Values on Mobilizing the Population*

Elites		1952	1953	1955	1957	1959	1961	1963	1965	1952-1957	1959-1965	All Years
PARTY	$N=$	(10)	(9)	(33)	(34)	(15)	(24)	(30)	(33)	(86)	(102)	(188)
Communist ideals		40	33	41	21	13	17	27	6	33.3	15.7	24.6
Exemplary behavior of the party		00	22	16	27	00	17	23	6	15.7	11.5	13.7
Not by bourgeois influences		20	22	16	15	13	00	7	18	18.2	9.5	14.2
Patriotism/nationalism		20	11	12	15	7	4	13	3	14.5	6.7	10.7
Material incentives		20	00	3	12	40	34	17	36	8.7	31.5	20.2
Popular support		00	11	12	12	27	29	13	33	8.7	25.5	17.2
ECONOMIC	$N=$	(9)	(15)	(29)	(20)	(16)	(18)	(26)	(24)	(73)	(84)	(157)
Communist ideals		22	27	7	10	00	11	4	4	16.5	4.8	10.7
Exemplary party		00	00	7	10	00	00	00	00	4.3	00.0	2.2
Not bourgeois		33	00	00	15	00	6	00	4	12.0	2.5	7.3
Patriotism/nationalism		22	7	3	10	00	6	8	4	10.5	4.5	7.5
Material incentives		11	33	68	40	88	50	61	54	38.3	63.5	50.9
Popular support		11	33	14	15	13	28	27	33	18.3	25.0	21.7
LEGAL	$N=$	(10)	(12)	(19)	(20)	(11)	(22)	(21)	(21)	(61)	(75)	(136)
Communist ideals		40	33	16	15	18	9	10	5	26.0	10.5	18.3
Exemplary party		00	17	11	10	00	5	5	5	9.5	2.5	6.0
Not bourgeois		20	8	00	5	00	00	00	00	8.3	00.0	4.2
Patriotism/nationalism		10	00	5	5	00	00	00	5	5.0	3.8	4.4
Material incentives		20	25	47	25	27	50	48	57	29.3	45.3	37.3
Popular support		10	17	21	40	55	36	28	33	22.0	38.0	30.3

Table 7.1.—Continued

Elites		1952	1953	1955	1957	1959	1961	1963	1965	1952-1957	1959-1965	All Years
MILITARY	N=	(—)	(—)	(28)	(37)	(27)	(28)	(35)	(29)	(65)	(119)	(184)
Communist ideals		—	—	22	14	15	22	26	20	17.5	20.8	19.2
Exemplary party		—	—	14	14	15	11	3	00	8.5	4.5	6.5
Not bourgeois		—	—	29	35	41	29	26	41	32.0	34.3	33.2
Patriotism/nationalism		—	—	29	38	22	22	35	24	33.5	26.0	29.8
Material incentives		—	—	00	00	4	7	00	3	00.0	3.5	1.8
Popular support		—	—	7	11	11	11	9	10	9.0	11.3	10.2
LITERARY	N=	(13)	(17)	(19)	(20)	(37)	(22)	(23)	(25)	(69)	(107)	(176)
Communist ideals		46	35	37	45	30	27	13	24	40.8	23.5	32.2
Exemplary party		00	18	32	10	8	5	4	4	15.0	5.3	10.2
Not bourgeois		31	30	16	10	24	27	17	20	21.5	22.0	21.8
Patriotism/nationalism		8	18	00	10	8	5	9	8	9.0	7.5	8.3
Material incentives		8	00	11	20	19	18	35	28	9.5	25.0	17.3
Popular support		8	00	5	5	11	18	22	16	4.5	16.8	10.7
TOTAL	N=	(42)	(53)	(128)	(131)	(106)	(114)	(135)	(132)	(354)	(487)	(841)

* level of significance of chi squares:

1952-57
Pty × Eco: $p < .001$
Pty × Leg: $p < .01$
Pty × Mil: $p < .001$
Pty × Lit : p not sig.

1959-65
Pty × Eco: $p < .001$
Pty × Leg: $p < .001$
Pty × Mil: $p < .001$
Pty × Lit : p not sig.

Over Time
Pty : $p < .001$
Eco: $p < .001$
Leg: $p < .001$
Mil: p not sig.
Lit : $p < .01$

nist ideals," the "exemplary behavior of the Party," opposition to "bourgeois influences," and appeals to "patriotism"—shows a decline, while the two instrumental values—"material incentives" and efforts to gain "popular support"—show a substantial increase. In the early period, 17% of the Party's total is devoted to instrumental values, 57% in the later. This instrumental trend is illustrated by Table 7.2 in a comparison

Table 7.2.   The Party's Dominant Values on How Best To Mobilize the Population

1952-57		1959-65		All Years	
communist ideals	33%	material incentives	32%	communist ideals	25%
not bourg. influences	18%	popular support	26%	material incentives	20%
exemplary Party	16%	communist ideals	16%	popular support	17%
% of Total	67%		74%		62%

of the Party's dominant orientation over time. The Party's instrumental trend compares favorably with that of the Specialists, and as will be shown, the difference between elites is primarily one of emphasis.

As was the case on the category tapping elite priorities on resource allocation, the *apparatchiki* favors a more balanced set of values than do any of the specialist elites, (e.g., for All-Years every option is in double figures), once again suggesting that the Party's orientation is more general than that of the specialist elites, in turn indicating that the Party is more responsive to the system as a whole than are any of the specialist elites.

The economic elite

In both periods the economic elite manifests the most instrumental orientation of all the elites. In the early period, 56% of its total is devoted to "material incentives" and "popular support," and in the later period the percentage rises to 89%. We find in Table 7.3 that in every year from 1953 through 1965, the economic elite's primary value is "material incentives," and its dominant orientation toward the population reflects this commitment as well. In 1959-65 "popular support" ranks second with 25%, giving instrumental values 89% of the economic elite's total.

When compared to the Party, it becomes clear that a major issue of contention between the *apparatchiki* and economic elite in the early

Table 7.3. The Economic Elite's Dominant Values on
How Best to Mobilize the Population

1952-57		1959-65		All Years	
material		material		material	
incentives	38%	incentives	64%	incentives	51%
popular support	18%			popular support	22%
communist					
ideals	17%				
% of Total	73%		64%		73%

period was the question of how to motivate the population. Whereas
the Party devoted 82% of its total to ideological incentives, the economic elite devoted over half its total to instrumental incentives. This
conflict was most pronounced in 1955 when ideological incentives received 85% of the Party's tally, but only 17% for the economic elite,
i.e., conflict, a mutual rejection of each other's policy orientation. In
1957 both the *apparatchiki* and economic elite adopted a more balanced stance, and throughout the later period the *apparatchiki* moves
toward a more instrumental posture. Thus, as was true on the resource
allocation category, the *apparatchiki* appears to have followed the economic elite's instrumental lead.

The legal elite

Following the pattern set by the economic elite, the legal elite
increasingly favors instrumental incentives for mobilizing the population. In devoting over three-quarters of its total to instrumental values,
the legal elite, as is the case with the economic elite, is appreciably
more instrumentally oriented than the *apparatchiki,* as shown in Table
7.4.

Table 7.4. The Legal Elite's Dominant Values on How
Best to Mobilize the Population

1952-57		1959-65		All Years	
material		material		material	
incentive	29%	incentive	45%	support	37%
communist		popular		popular	
ideals	26%	support	38%	support	30%
popular support	22%				
% of Total	77%		83%		67%

The military elite

The military's position as a pariah in the Soviet political system is strikingly demonstrated in its orientation to the population. As in its attitudinal orientation toward the Party's role and its priorities on resource allocation, the military elite consistently supports its primary commitment to military spending by rejecting instrumental incentives in favor of the less costly appeal to "patriotism" and ideological injunctions against "bourgeois influences." For All-Years "communist ideals" ranks third with 19% of the military's total (Table 7.5).

Table 7.5. The Military Elite's Dominant Values on How Best to Mobilize the Population

1952-57		1959-65		All Years	
patriotism	34%	*not* bourgeois	35%	*not* bourgeois	33%
not bourgeois	32%	patriotism	26%	patriotism	30%
% of Total	66%		61%		63%

While the military's dominant values are ideological, in fact more ideological oriented than is the Party, "patriotism" and opposition to "bourgeois influences" are *not* supported by the Party; both in fact are depreciated by the *apparatchiki* over time. If, as seems to be the case, the bourgeois tendencies decried by the military are the growing emphasis with "material incentives" and related efforts to gain "popular support," the military is as isolated from the *apparatchiki* as it is from the specialist elites. Note, e.g., the military's flat rejection of the "exemplary Party," 9% in 1952-57, 5% in 1959-65. Military opposition to instrumental incentives places the military elite outside the All-Elite mainstream.

The literary elite

On the question of how best to motivate the population the literary elite is faction ridden, so much so that there are few points of intra-elite consensus. In 1952-57 the literary elite's dominant values are ideological: "communist ideals" 41%, and opposition to "bourgeois influences" 22%. *Oktyabr* accounts for over half, 54%, of the literary's references to "communist ideals," and 59% of the elite's concern with "bourgeois influences." *Novy mir* is the most instrumentally oriented elite.

Over time the literary elite records a marked instrumental increase, yet the intra-elite factional differentiation remains. Although the literary elite's ideological values decline and instrumental values increase over time, "communist ideals" and opposition to "bourgeois influences" rank second and third in the elite's dominant value orientation. Both ideological values are the primary values of *Oktyabr*. This conservative journal accounts for over half of the literary elite's ideological values and *Novy mir* for over half of the elite's instrumental values.

The literary elite, when viewed as a single collective entity, is closest to the Party's values for All-Years; however, neither the conservative nor liberal factions of the literary elite is in tune with the *apparatchiki* in either period. *Oktyabr* appears to be threatened by the Party's tendency to sacrifice ideological for instrumental values, with only one ideological option—"the exemplary behavior of the Party"—showing a decline. Interestingly, the primary value articulated by *Oktyabr* is the injunction against "bourgeois influences." *Novy mir* more closely approximates the economic elite's orientation than that of either of the other literary factions or the Party. *Literaturnaya gazeta* occupies a middle position and more generally approximates the Party's values in both periods.

Party-specialist relations

Comparing *apparatchiki* to specialist elite value orientations on how best to motivate the population, Table 7.6 shows that the predicted in-

Table 7.6.   The Decline of Ideological Values on How Best To Mobilize the Population

Elites	1952-57	1959-65	% Point Decline Over Time
Party	82%	45%	−37
Economic	44%	13%	−31
Legal	49%	18%	−31
Military	93%	80%	−13
Literary	87%	59%	−28
Specialists	68%	43%	−25

crease in instrumental values over time is valid for all the elites. Each of the elites de-emphasizes ideological values over time. However, contrary to initial expectations, the *apparatchiki* is *not* the most ideologically oriented elite; in both periods the Party occupies a centrist position between the more instrumentally oriented economic and legal elites on the one side and the more ideologically oriented military and literary elites (primarily *Oktyabr*) on the other.

Since the Party's orientation toward the population is a mix of ideological and instrumental values, to measure the anticipated increase in
Party-elite conflict over time, the most meaningful indicator of accommodation and conflict on this question is derived from a comparison
of Party to elite dominant value orientations. As on the category tapping elite priorities on the question of resource allocation, conflict exists
when the percentage point difference between the *apparatchiki* and
elite is above the specialist elite's All-Year average; accommodation
exists when the level of disagreement is below the elite's All-Year average. Table 7.7 tallies the conflict/accommodation scores for each specialist elite. Plus signs denote the extent of conflict, minus signs the
extent of accommodation.

The anticipated increase in Party-elite conflict is not strongly supported for Specialists as an entity. Due to the Party's turnabout from
an ideological to an instrumental value orientation over time, each of
the specialist elites experiences a shift in Party-elite relations. The
economic and legal elites move from a state of conflict in the early
period to accommodation in the later period, suggesting that although
both elites are more instrumentally oriented than the Party in 1959-65,
apparatchiki and elite orientations are basically consensual. The reverse
is true for the military and literary elites, both of whom were in agreement with the Party's early commitment to ideological values, but
neither of which followed the Party's transition to a more instrumental
orientation. Unlike the economic and legal elites, the military and literary elites moved from accommodation in 1952-57 to conflict in 1959-65.
As noted in the discussion of the military elite, this conflict represents a rejection of the Party's commitment to material incentives. The
literary elite's ideological orientation, more correctly that of *Oktyabr*,
appears to be rooted more in a traditional attachment to general ideological values than to any specific orientation or claim on resources.

The data suggest—the military elite withstanding—that a dominant
thrust of the post-Stalin period is the growing commitment to instrumental incentives in motivating the population. The Party's orientation
on this category is decidedly in this direction. To what extent, if any,
the *apparatchiki* conceives of its position in the political arena as dependent on the population's material well-being is a moot question.
Data relevant to the issue are suggestive but not conclusive. For example, in the 1959-65 period, the Party's primary values on mobilizing the
population are "material incentives" and efforts to gain "popular
support." This orientation is given substance on the earlier category tapping Party values on the allocation of resources in which the *apparatchiki* devotes 23% of its 1959-65 total to agriculture, 18% to light

Table 7.7. Party-Elite Conflict/Accommodation: Dominant Values on How Best to Mobilize the Population

Elites	1952	1953	1955	1957	1959	1961	1963	1965	1952-1957	1959-1965	All Years
Economic	−30	+42	+53	− 4	− 1	−46	+27	−45	+15	−16	− 1
Legal	−46	− 2	+48	+28	− 5	−23	+25	−25	+ 7	− 7	000
Military	—	—	−31	−20	+17	+17	− 1	+20	−26	+13	−13
Literary	−27	−30	−24	+10	+22	+20	+26	+ 1	−18	+17	− 1
Specialists	−34	+ 3	+12	+ 4	+ 8	− 8	+19	−12	− 6	+ 2	− 4

industry, and 13% to living standard, for a 54% commitment to instrumental priorities. However, on the category tapping the Party's role perceptions, the Party places only 13% value on its responsibility for raising the "standard of living," ranking it below "communism," "economic achievement," and "scientific advance." While scientific and economic development, or for that matter "communism," do not preclude improvements in the standard of living, in fact, have promoted it, the economic, legal and literary elites all cite "standard of living" as a primary value, indicating that it is qualitatively different from the less direct methods favored by the *apparatchiki* for increasing mass consumption. Perhaps the best indicator of this difference in orientation is the Party's unwillingness to invest adequate capital in agriculture (23% in 1959-65 for the *apparatchiki*, a 38% average for the economic, legal, and literary elites). It would appear, then, that the economic, legal, and literary elites are more consistent than the Party apparat in their commitment to improve the lot of Ivan Ivanovich.

Summary: Elite Orientations

At the outset of this discussion of *gruppovshchina*, (groupism), three sociological conditions were set forth to judge whether the specialist elites constitute groups. The first standard, that the elites must perceive themselves as a group, was supported (in Table 3.3) as each elite shows a significant increase in group self-consciousness over time— Specialists, e.g., recording an 111% increase in 1959-65 over the early period. The second condition of groupism, that the elites be recognized as groups by the other elites, was still more strongly supported (Tables 3.4 and 3.5) with an 108% average increase in ascribed group status over time. The final sociological condition, that the specialist elites manifest a set of values which are distinct from those of the *apparatchiki*, specifically, more instrumental than the Party's, was analyzed in terms of each elite's attitudes toward five major problems of the post-Stalin period. The data suggest that the Soviet political system is not an ideal-type Party dominant system—*apparatchiki*-specialist elite attitudinal conflict, not accommodation, characterizes the political system. Moreover, the specialist elites show a discernible tendency over time to reject those values which underpin Party dominance and support those values which tend to promote elite participation and group cohesion.

In the analysis of Party values it is apparent that over time the Party moves from a strong ideological position to a more balanced mix of ideological and instrumental values. If it is valid to assume (and the data generally support the assumption) that the *apparatchiki* tends to favor those values which support its dominance in the political system, by comparing *apparatchiki* to elite accommodation/conflict scores on all five issue-oriented categories, it is possible to gain a measure of the extent to which the specialist elites are developing a more instrumental (participatory) orientation over time.

In Table 7.8 each specialist elite's accommodation/conflict score is tabulated for all issue-oriented categories combined. Conflict characterizes the post-Stalin period. Party-Specialist orientations are in conflict in every year but 1952, and over time the level of conflict increases by 118%. Each specialist elite manifests a marked increase in conflict in 1959-65 over 1952-57, the Specialists showing a threefold increase.

While *apparatchiki*-elite conflict is the hallmark of the post-Stalin period, the issues of conflict vary over time. In Table 7.9, Party-Specialist accommodation/conflict scores are tabulated for each of the issue-oriented categories. On the two categories which focus on the problem of specialist elite autonomy (What the Role of the Party Should Be and Who Is Responsible for Socialization), Party-Specialist conflict is high and more than doubles in intensity over time. On the categories which center on the relationship between the elites and the population (The Mobilization of the Population and The Allocation of Resources) the overall trend is toward accommodation as all the elites but the military show a marked tendency to agree on a basic commitment toward improvements in the standard of living through material incentives and heavier investments in agriculture and light industry. It would, therefore, appear that *the apparatchiki is pursuing a dual course: while tending to develop a more instrumental orientation vis-a-vis the population, the apparatchiki is simultaneously attempting to maintain its dominance over the specialist elites by means of ideological controls.* Whatever the long range effects, the immediate result is intensified *apparatchiki*-elite conflict.

The second pattern which emerges from the data pinpoints the year 1963 as a time of Party-elite "crisis." *In 1963 all the Specialist elites record an increase in conflict with the apparatchiki.* In 1963 each specialist elite manifests a level of conflict above its All-Year average and all five categories are issues of contention above their All-Year average. The year 1963 is also, it will be recalled, the most conflict-ridden year on the participatory categories, suggesting that for the first time in the post-Stalin period, the specialist elites challenge *apparatchiki* dominance on all fronts—pressuring for a greater role in policy and decision making and rejecting the Party's values on the major political questions of the day.

Table 7.8. Party-Elite Accommodation/Conflict on All Issue-Oriented Categories Combined

Elites	1952	1953	1955	1957	1959	1961	1963	1965	1952-1957	1959-1965	All Years
Economic	−10	+23	+46	+10	+27	+17	+41	+24	+17	+26	+22
Legal	−38	+ 3	+18	−10	−12	+ 4	+18	+11	− 7	+ 5	− 1
Military	—	—	− 7	+16	+38	+13	+40	+18	+ 5	+27	+16
Literary	+ 4	+15	+20	+ 8	+13	+20	+30	+21	+12	+21	+17
Specialists	−14	+13	+19	+ 6	+17	+14	+32	+16	+ 6	+20	+13

Table 7.9. Party-Specialist Accommodation/Conflict on the Issue-Oriented Categories

Categories	1952	1953	1955	1957	1959	1961	1963	1965	1952-1957	1959-1965	All Years
Socialization	+12	+ 9	+20	+16	+57	+30	+52	+52	+10	+48	+29
Party's role is	−18	+19	−26	−27	− 7	+11	+ 1	+29	−14	+ 8	− 1
Party's role should be	− 5	+19	+75	+29	+17	+19	+83	+63	+37	+46	+40
Resource allocation	−27	+17	+15	+ 8	+ 9	+17	+ 6	−40	+13	− 8	+ 5
Mobilization of population	−34	+ 3	+12	+ 4	+ 8	− 8	+19	−12	− 6	+ 2	− 4
Totals	−14	+13	+19	+ 6	+17	+14	+32	+16	+ 6	+20	+13

The effects of this 1963 crisis in Party-elite relations on Khrushchev's ouster cannot be directly deduced from the data, although three findings are relevant to the question. First, throughout 1959-65 the level of *apparatchiki*-elite conflict is high, reaching a peak in the year immediately preceding the First Secretary's fall. Second, in 1963 the major indicators of *gruppovshchina* show a marked increase over the immediate 1959-61 period, e.g., for Specialists a 19% increase in self-consciousness, a 42% increase in ascribed group status, and an increased emphasis on the role of "occupational groups" in elite socialization. Finally, whatever the specialists' role in Khrushchev's fall, no dramatic shift in Party-elite relations resulted in 1965 from the change; the level of conflict is not appreciably diminished from 1963 to 1965. The root causes of Party-elite conflict—the Party's resistance to the specialist elites' thrust for greater autonomy and participation—continues unabated through 1965.

Are the specialist elites groups? In terms of the data all the sociological conditions of group consciousness are met. Prudence, however, demands that an affirmative answer be qualified. First, the data deal with elite attitudes, not behavior. Second, without studies of elite group influence on policy decisions, the data could be, *should be*, interpreted as representing tendencies toward group consciousness rather than the achievement of group status.[2] These disclaimers acknowledged, an attempt is made in the concluding chapter to chart the major trends in *apparatchiki*-elite relations in the post-Stalin period.

---

[2] In addition to the works on group theory cited in the introduction to Part Two, see Philip D. Stewart, *Political Power in the Soviet Union* (New York: The Bobbs-Merrill Co., 1968), and the volume edited by Allen Kassov, *Prospects For Soviet Society* (New York: Praeger, 1968), especially the articles by Jeremy Azrael, Sidney Ploss, and Thomas Wolfe.

8 Conclusion: Party-Elite Relations in the Post-Stalin Period

In *The Governmental Process,* David Truman distinguishes between active and potential interest groups.[1] According to Truman, interest groups, "on the basis of one or more shared values," make claims upon the system through the institutions of government. A potential interest group *aspires* to press its claim on the government. The distinction is an empirical one. Does the group hold common values? Is it successful in influencing policy?

As shown in the chapters on elite orientations, the specialist elites develop a set of values over time which are distinct from and in conflict with the values of the *apparatchiki.* In the analysis of participatory attitudes the evidence clearly demonstrated that the elites aspire to a greater role in the decision-making process. By all counts, then, the specialist elites are, at minimum, potential interest groups. The crucial question is, of course, are the elites active interest groups?

The data do not permit us to measure elite influence on policy decisions. It is possible, however, to determine the ex-

---

[1] (New York: Alfred A. Knopf, 1958), esp. pp. 501-507.

tent to which the elites give the appearance of an active rather than a potential interest group. Toward this end three types of Party-elite relationships may be operationally discerned:

1. The Specialist Elite as *Transmission Belt*
   a. The *apparatchiki* and elite basically agree on the major policy questions of the day.
   b. The specialist elite does not manifest participatory attitudes; in operational terms, the elite scores in the 1.0 to 2.4 range on the participatory categories, a level of participation in which the *apparatchiki* dominates the policy-making arena.

2. The Specialist Elite as *Potential Interest Group*
   a. The *apparatchiki* and elite are in conflict over policy, i.e., the specialist elite articulates a more instrumental policy orientation than the *apparatchiki*.
   b. The elite aspires to a more participatory role but fails to develop a participatory orientation; in operational terms, the specialist elite scores in the 2.5-2.9 range (the Party's "mini-max" boundaries) where it may be better able to exert some influence on policy decisions but is not "pressing" forcefully its claims on the *apparatchiki*.

3. The Specialist Elite as *Active Interest Group*.
   a. The *apparatchiki* and elite are in significant conflict over policy questions.
   b. The specialist elite manifests a participatory (3.0-5.0) set of attitudes—the elite is in an attitudinal position vis-a-vis the *apparatchiki* whereby it is thought to be better able to actively pursue its interests.

The operational distinctions my be reduced to two conditions:

Party-Elite Relationship		Level of Elite Participation	+	Party-Elite Policy Accommodation/Conflict
Transmission Belt	=	1.0-2.4	+	policy accommodation
Potential Interest Group	=	2.5-2.9	+	policy conflict
Active Interest Group	=	3.0-5.0	+	intense policy conflict

To demark the changing patterns of Party-elite relations over time, each elite's scores on all the categories are tabulated.

I. Party-Economic Elite Relations

From work bench to planning table—throughout the economic structure—the *apparatchiki* and economic elite share a responsibility for Soviet industrial development. As Fainsod notes,

... the preoccupation of the top leadership with the problems of production has made the technical and managerial intelligensia an
indispensible adjunct of power and given its members an increasingly significant role in the directive apparatus of the Soviet state.[2]

This interlocking responsibility promotes a conflict-ridden Party-
economic elite relationship. The problems of production, most notably
the drive for greater productivity, lower costs, efficiency, and of late the
campaign to improve the quality of goods, create cross organizational
pressures. The need for economic rationality

... leads to emphasis on one-man management and a reinforcement
of the authority and prerequisites of the managerial class. The
[Party leadership's] anxiety about loyalty induces strenuous efforts
to assimilate the technical and managerial intelligensia into the Party
and involves reliance on the Party and police controls to hold the
power of the managerial elite in check.[3]

Party-economic elite conflict, judged by its endurance throughout the
Soviet period, is inherent in the system. To what extent the economic
elite appears to have developed into an interest group is the question
posed here. Utilizing the economic elite's totals on the participatory
and policy categories, the general pattern of elite development is
illustrated in Figure 3.

The economic elite runs the gamut of Party-elite relations. Under
Stalin in 1952 and again in 1957 following Khrushchev's victory and
economic reorganization, the economic elite is a satellite, a "transmission belt," of the *apparatchiki*. In 1953 the perceived levels of participation and conflict climb, propelling the economic elite into the
role of a "potential interest group." In 1955 and throughout the 1959-65
period the economic elite meets the operational criteria of an "active
interest group"—moving beyond the Party's "mini-max" range of
2.5 to 2.9 on the participatory categories and adopting an instrumental
policy orientation which challenges the dominance of the *apparatchiki*.

In 1952 the economic elite is in basic agreement with the *apparatchiki* on the essentials of an ideological political system. Only a modicum of Party-elite conflict exists. As the increase in economic elite
participation and Party-elite conflict attest, Stalin's death in 1953 apparently freed the economic elite to exert itself more forcefully. Conflict
centered in two areas: first, the elite pressed its claim for control at
the production level—scoring 2.5 on "Who is responsible for decision-

---

[2] Merle Fainsod, *How Russia is Ruled* (Cambridge: Harvard University Press,
1963), p. 503.
[3] *Ibid.*, p. 504.

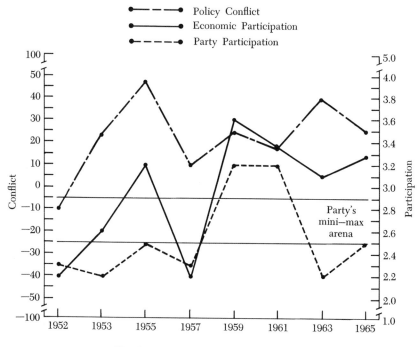

Fig. 3.   Party-Economic Elite Relations

making" and 4.0 on "Who should make decisions." The second field
of contention centered on the Party's role vis-a-vis the population
where the economic elite began to develop a distinctly more instrumental orientation, reflected in a +19 level of conflict on the question
of resource allocations, +42 on how best to mobilize the population,
and culminating in sharp conflict, +42, on the question of the role
of the Party. In 1953 the economic elite meets the conditions of a
"potential interest group."

In 1955 Party-economic elite relations are in crisis. Both the *apparatchiki* and economic elite adopt mutually exclusive positions, resulting in conflict on all five participatory and all five policy categories.
The Party demands a dominant role in the political arena, 2.2, and
strikes an ideological position on all the policy issues. The economic
elite challenges Party dominance with a 3.2 participatory average
and supports this thrust with an instrumental policy orientation. The
economic elite manifests a remarkably coherent set of attitudes to
support its role as an "active interest group." To cite merely those
values which directly undermine Party dominance, the elite opts for
a participatory role in policy-making, averages 3.8 on the decision-

making categories (the near exclusion of the *apparatchiki* from the managerial level), denies "historical consciousness" and "socialist democracy" as legitimate bases of Party rule, and challenges the Party's claim of responsibility in elite socialization with a 75% emphasis on instrumental agents. In sum, the *apparatchiki* and economic elite are locked in a conflict relationship from which there appears to be little room for compromise.

With Khrushchev's victory in 1957 the economic elite is again reduced to a satellite relationship vis-a-vis the *apparatchiki*. The level of participation falls from 3.2 to 2.2, and the Party successfully dampens economic resistance to its policy line. As in 1952-53, however, telltale signs of conflict point out areas of contention: +36 on what the Party's role should be, +9 on resource allocation priorities, and +7 on elite socialization. Party-economic conflict, although not strong, +10, nonetheless exists and as scores in the later period suggest the Party's "victory" in 1957 was not long standing.

Judged by our indicators, throughout the 1959-65 period the economic elite plays an "active interest group role"—in each of the later years the level of participation and conflict is in the instrumental range. In 1959 and 1961 Party-economic elite relations undergo two marked shifts from the earlier period. (1) The *apparatchiki* accedes to the economic elite's demand for a participatory role in the local decision-making arena but retains its commitment to supremacy in policy-making with a 2.5 average in both 1959 and 1961. With their role in the decision-making arena seemingly recognized, the economic elite and to a lesser extent all the specialist elites move to gain a voice in the making of policy, the economic elite averaging 3.0 on the policy-making categories in 1959 and 3.2 in 1961. This move to the national level represents a qualitative change in *apparatchiki*-elite attitudinal relations. (2) The second shift occurs on the categories tapping elite relations to the population. The Party reverses its 1952-57 commitment to ideological incentives and apparently co-opts the instrumental orientation of the economic, legal, and literary elite.

The year 1963 is, like 1955, a year of crisis in Party-economic elite relations. The Party reverts to an ideological position on all the categories. The immediate result is Party-elite conflict: the economic elite maintains its participatory attitudes with a 3.1 average (the *apparatchiki* retreating to 2.2), and continues to articulate an instrumental policy orientation. The level of conflict is significant on four of the five policy issues, averaging out to +41. Whatever the precipitating causes for the Party's turnabout—whether it stemmed from the agricultural crisis, the Cuban missile crisis, problems with Chairman Mao, dissension within the Politburo, the low rate of industrial growth, or the growing influence of the specialist elites in the political arena—Party-economic elite conflict reached crisis proportions. Unlike 1955 when the economic elite stood alone and the *apparatchiki* enjoyed the support of the military, in 1963 all the specialist elites (the economic and military most forcefully) appear to actively challenge the dominance of the *apparatchiki* in the political arena.

Khrushchev's ouster as First Secretary in 1964 does not dramatically affect Party-elite relations in 1965. The level of conflict declines but nonetheless remains significantly intense. As seen in Figure 3, the level of Party-economic elite conflict on the policy issues declines from +41 in 1963 to +24 in 1965, largely as a result of the Party's return to a more instrumental posture vis-a-vis the population. Basically unchanged and a point of sharp conflict is the Party's commitment to its dominance in the policy and decision making process. The Party's score on all participation categories combined is 2.5 in 1965, representing an attempt once again to enforce "'mini-max" boundaries on the specialist elites. The economic elite's 1965 score is 3.3, a bid for relative equality with the *apparatchiki* in the political arena. Between the Party's plan for limited specialist elite participation and the economic elite's demand for co-participant status is a gulf which neither Khrushchev nor the new leaders find bridgeable.

II. Party-Legal Elite Relations

Under Stalin, Soviet law and the legal machinery were adjuncts of administrative policy. The Party's theoretical position (most clearly articulated by Vyshinsky) emphasized the subordination of law to Party policy. The use of the past tense in describing the Party's attitude and behavior toward law is necessitated by the profound post-Stalin developments in "socialist legality."[4] On the one hand the Party's commitment to scientific progress, economic advance, and to the consumer demands regularity, and regularity in turn demands legal norms.[5] On the ideological side, however, Party dominance is in part supported by the Party's ability to supercede law and by-pass routinized procedures, standards, and legal norms. As Leonard Shapiro notes, "the main obstacle to the development of the rule of law [in the Soviet Union] is, as it always has been, the vested interest of the

---

[4] For a review of post-Stalin legal developments, see the Special Issue, "Law and Legality in the USSR," *Problems of Communism*, Vol. XIV, 2 (March-April 1965).
[5] *Ibid.*, pp. 2-7.

Party apparatus in arbitrary illegality."[6] At root, then *apparatchiki*-legal elite relations are a blend of accommodation and conflict—cooperation in the creation of law for the maintenance and development of the system, counterbalanced by potential legal elite opposition to the Party's need to step outside legal standards if it is to maintain its dominance in the system.[7] The aim here is not to determine the influence of jurists on the Soviet legislative process (presently an impossible task) but to take a more preliminary step, namely to gain a measure of the extent to which the legal elite has developed the attitudinal structure to meet our operational criteria of an active interest group. Figure 4 illustrates the legal elite's scores on all categories.

The legal elite progresses from a "transmission belt" role in 1952 and 1953 to a "potential interest group" in 1955, 1957, and 1959 to a weak "active interest group" in the years from 1961 through 1965. While the level of *apparatchiki*-legal elite conflict is less than that existing between the Party and economic elite, high levels of conflict occur

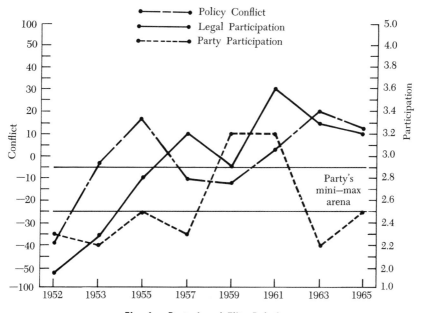

Fig. 4. Party-Legal Elite Relations

---

[6] *Ibid.*, p. 7.

[7] On the question of opposition to the Party within the legal elite see Harold Berman, "The Struggle of Soviet Jurists Against A Return to Stalinist Terror," *Slavic Review*, XII (June, 1963), pp. 314-320.

in 1955, 1961, 1963 and 1965. It is only in the later period, however, that the legal elite manages to support its instrumental orientation with participatory scores and a show of group consciousness.

By all indicators in the data for 1952, the legal profession is an administrative arm of the Stalinist system: it ranks as the most ideologically oriented elite (-38 on the policy categories, 1.9 on the participatory categories). Its status as a transmission belt is also reflected on the measures of group consciousness (2 self references, no ascribed group references). With the death of Stalin and police chief Lavrenti Beria, and the collective leadership's emphasis on "socialist legality" in 1953, the legal elite shows signs of activity. Conflict on policy questions rises to +3, participation to 2.3, group self-consciousness increases, and the other elites begin to perceive the legal profession as a more prominent group, ranking it third behind the *apparatchiki* and economic elite. Still a "satellite" of the Party, the legal elite begins to manifest the rudimentary characteristics of a distinct actor in the political system.

In 1955, legal elite participatory scores climb to 2.8 and Party-elite conflict to +18. As a "potential interest group" the major issues of contention center on two related questions: first, the legal elite moves to secure a position in the decision-making arena (3.3 on who should participate); and second, the legal elite articulates an instrumental orientation toward the population (+48 on resource allocation, +48 on mobilizing the population, and a +84 level of conflict on what the role of the Party should be). The legal elite's commitment to instrumental incentives throughout the post-Stalin period apparently is directly related to its campaign for "socialist legality," for both are premised on the belief that the regime's goals ("communism" broadly defined) are attainable through instrumental incentives and related efforts to gain popular support.

The years from 1957 through 1959 are a period of Party-legal elite cooperation. At the 20th Party Congress Khrushchev's denunciation of Stalin officially committed the Party to "socialist legality," resulting in the legal elite's active participation in the formulation of the "Fundamental Principles of Criminal Legislation." Party-elite policy conflict declined as the *apparatchiki* adopted a more instrumental position vis-a-vis the population. The decline in conflict scores suggests that the legal elite viewed the Party as an instrument of reform. Note, for example, that the legal elite is in basic agreement with the *apparatchiki* on the role of the Party (−100 in 1957, −79 in 1959), and, more importantly, on what should be the role of the Party (+ 5 and − 19 respectively).

This spirit of cooperation was shattered in 1961 with passage of the special decrees of 1961-62—the anti-parasite legislation, reintroduction of the death penalty for economic crimes, and the renewed emphasis on the Stalinist concept of crime as a "survival of capitalism." In the eyes of the legal elite, it would appear, the Party violated the 1958 reforms.[8] The period of close Party-legal elite cooperation was over. From 1961 through 1965, Soviet jurists openly express disillusion with the Party's retreat from 1958 and speak out against the persistence of Stalinist attitudes and practices.

Throughout the 1961-65 period the legal elite meets the *minimal* operational requisites of an "active interest group": the legal elite manifests a participatory set of attitudes, maintains an instrumental policy orientation, and meets the conditions of group consciousness. Attitudinal conflict permeates the whole spectrum of Party-legal elite relations as the legal profession complements its policy demands on the Party with participatory scores in both the policy and decision-making arenas.

III. Party-Military Elite Relations

As both this and other recent studies show, *apparatchiki*-military relations in the post-Stalin period are conflict-ridden.[9] The level of Party-military conflict is high, the highest among all the specialists for the 1959-65 period, and shows a four-fold increase over time. The military's scores on all the categories are plotted in Figure 5.

Like the other specialist elites, a major source of *apparatchiki*-military conflict is rooted in the specialist elite's quest for a more participatory role in the political arena and a greater degree of professional autonomy vs. Party dominance. Unlike the other elites, however, the military is threatened by the 1959-65 trends toward a more instrumental regime-society relationship. Whereas the *apparatchiki*, economic, legal, and literary elites are moving toward accommodation on the questions of the allocation of resources and the mobilization of the population, the military stands alone in its continued support for the traditional priorities of heavy industrial and military expenditures. This conflict is reflected on all the categories as the military makes a concerted effort to support its claims by undermining the dominance of the *apparatchiki*.

---

[8] See Kazimierz Grzybowski, "Soviet Criminal Law," *op. cit.*, pp. 53-62, for a discussion of the post-1961 disillusionment of Soviet jurists.

[9] Particularly, see Matthew P. Gallagher "Military Manpower: A Case Study," *Problems of Communism*, Vol. XIII, 3 (May-June 1964), pp. 53-62; Thomas W. Wolfe, *op. cit.*, pp. 1-19; and Roman Kolkowicz, *op. cit.*, pp. 11-79.

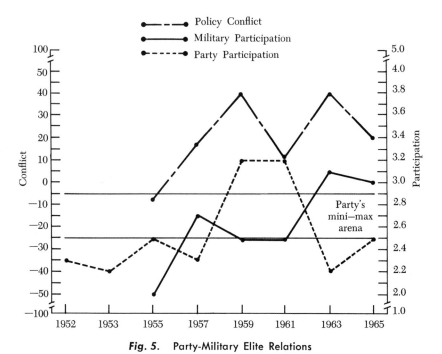

Fig. 5.   Party-Military Elite Relations

In 1955 the Party and military basically agree on a wide range of perspectives and attitudes which reflect a common commitment to the primacy of heavy industry and a strong military budget. In 1955 the *apparatchiki* is locked in conflict with the economic elite, and it is readily apparent from the scores that a Party-military coalition is operative against the consumerism of Malenkov. In return for military support against the economic elite, Khrushchev adopts a pro-military (and no-doubt pro-*apparatchiki*) posture, best exemplified by their joint commitment to the traditional priorities on the resource allocation category.

As long as the *apparatchiki* supported the military elite's interest in budgetary priorities, the military was apparently content with a modicum of participation; however, as the figures for 1957 so clearly demonstrate, following the defeat of Malenkov in 1955-57, the First Secretary reversed his position, co-opted the economic elite's values on the allocation of resources, and turned on the military elite. The immediate effect of the Party's turnabout is *apparatchiki*-military conflict on both the participatory and policy issues. The military elite immediately appears as a "potential interest group" as it presses its policy demands on the Party by means of higher scores on the policy and decision-making categories.

As shown in the earlier analysis of the military elite's 1957 attitudes (Table 2.16), the year is made up of two distinct periods. While Marshal Zhukov was Minister of Defense the military ranked as an "active interest group." Under Zhukov's leadership the military appears to have successfully challenged the dominance of the *apparatchiki* and pressed for a decisive voice in military affairs, scoring 3.6 on who should make policy and 4.4 (the virtual exclusion of the *apparatchiki*) on who should make decisions, for an average on all the participatory categories of 3.3. With Khrushchev's victory over the "anti-Party group" in mid-1957, the First Secretary removed Zhukov from the Ministry of Defense and the Party Central Committee and reforged Party controls over the military. The military elite was quickly reduced to a "satellite" role, averaging 1.9 on the participatory categories for the remainder of 1957. The ease with which Khrushchev ousted Marshal Zhukov and reestablished Party control attests to the power of the Party apparatus to thwart a direct challenge to its dominance. As the data for the 1959-65 period suggest and events were to prove, the Party's victory was shortlived.

In strengthening the mechanisms of political control over the military, Khrushchev exploited existing cleavages within the military elite and promoted the so-called "Stalingrad Group"—those top military officers who had served with Khrushchev in the battle of Stalingrad in 1942-43—into positions of leadership.[10] This symbiotic relationship was premised on an assumed union of *apparatchiki* and military interests. It collapsed as the military leadership gradually came to realize that Khrushchev's policy line, in particular his consumer orientation and demand for political controls, was a major threat to the professional and institutional interests of the military elite. The emergence of the military as a self-conscious "active interest group" progressed in two discernable stages, the first from 1959-1961, the second from 1963-1965.

Beginning in 1959 signs of tension appeared within the military leadership and the Stalingrad Group became internally divided:

> The issues that caused this polarization of loyalties and interests in the Stalingrad Group were Khrushchev's sweeping reforms of strategic doctrine and of the socio-political culture of the officer corps, as well as his economic policies, which effectively discriminated against the less important [and less costly] sectors of the military establishment in favor of the strategically vital ones. The split in the Stalingrad Group was essentially a crisis of primary loyalty in which

---

[10] See Kolkowicz, *op. cit.*, pp. 220-281, for an analysis of Khrushchev's relationship to the Group.

members had to choose between their professional and institutional interests . . . and unquestioning loyalty to their benefactor and Party leader.[11]

Gradually, as the impact of Khrushchev's policy line became clear (in 1960, e.g., Khrushchev proposed a drastic cut in the conventional armed forces and cashiered 250,000 officers out of the service), a "military" viewpoint—a general dissatisfaction with the course of Party policy and a specific antipathy towards Khrushchev—matured. The Cuban missile crisis galvanized the military into an "active interest group": participatory attitudes climbed from 2.5 in 1959-61 to 3.1 in 1963, *apparatchiki*-military policy conflict to + 40, and both group self-consciousness and ascribed group status reflect corresponding increases. Most interesting are the military's participation scores on the policy-making categories, 3.3 on who is responsible for policy-making, 3.2 on who should be responsible. This is the first time since Zhukov that the military scored in the participatory range in the policy-making arena. In 1963, then, Party-military elite relations are in "crisis" as the two elite's adopt mutually exclusive positions on both the participation and policy categories.

In 1965, although the level of conflict has abated somewhat, the military elite leads all elites in attitudinal conflict with the *apparatchiki*: participation is 3.0 and Party-elite conflict on both the participatory and policy categories is significant. Little is changed in the military elite's relationship to the Party, largely due to the fact that new Party leadership is pursuing Khrushchev's instrumental course vis-a-vis the population and attempting to maintain its dominance in the political arena. "Khrushchevism without Khrushchev" is no solution to *apparatchiki*-military conflict, and as the 1965 scores attest the military elite is apparently engaged in an attempt to overturn the Party's post-1957 policy line.

IV. Party-Literary Elite Relations

Party-literary relations in the post-Stalin period are characterized by conflict, episodic conflict, periods of Party suppression followed by "thaws."[12] The struggle, whatever its guise (whether fought over the issue of "socialist realism," "truthfulness in art," "formalism," "abstractionism," or "the cult of the individual") is not merely or even primarily

---

[11] *Ibid.*, p. 223.

[12] Secondary material on the Soviet literary is extensive, although for the most part focused on individual writers and specific works. The sources found to be

an affair of the arts. At root it is the same problem which plagues *apparatchiki*-elite relations in general—the struggle between Party dominance and elite autonomy.

As noted in the earlier analysis of literary elite attitudes, intra-elite factional differences appear on most categories and support the often made distinction between "conservative" and "liberal" wings within the literary intelligentsia. Unfortunately, because of the low *N* for any one faction, it is impossible to chart Party-factional relations. Hence, the literary elite in all its variation is treated as a single entity. What is assumed, then, is that the "conservative" attitudes expressed in *Oktyabr* are balanced out by the "liberal" positions articulated in *Novy mir*. Insofar as the assumption is valid, the results tap a centrist position for the literary elite.

Problems arise in interpreting the data, for frequently a success for the liberals is a setback for the conservatives. For example, "thaws" and "freezes" in Party-literary relations tends to follow the on-again off-again process of de-Stalinization. The liberal intelligentsia actively support the campaigns, since de-Stalinization undermines "Stalin's heirs" in the *apparatchiki* and cultural bureaucracy and works to loosen literary controls.[13] Retreats favor the conservatives in tending to emphasize ideological orthodoxy. In the period from 1961 through 1963 this thaw-freeze process reached a peak and may serve to illustrate the effects on the liberal and conservative factions.

Khrushchev, following the 22nd Party Congress in October 1961, embarked on another de-Stalinization campaign, apparently intending to uproot resistance within the *apparatchiki* and elites to his "economics over politics" line. The liberal faction aided in the campaign. Solzhenitsyn's *One Day in the Life of Ivan Denisovich*, with Khrushchev's personal approval, was published in *Novy mir*, Yevtushenko's "Stalin's Heirs" in *Pravda*, and control of the Moscow Writers' Union passed into the hands of the liberals. In late 1962 and early 1963 Khrushchev was forced to beat a retreat:[14] the anti-Stalin campaign withered away, and the "metal eaters" resisted the First Secretary's instrumental eco-

---

most helpful in analyzing the literary elite are: Priscilla Johnson, *op. cit.*, pp. 1-89; Vera S. Dunham, "Insights from Soviet Literature," *Journal of Conflict Resolution*, Vol. VIII, No. 4 (Dec. 1964), pp. 386-410; Max Hayward and Edward Crowley, eds., *Soviet Literature in the Sixties* (New York: Praeger, 1964); Max Hayward and Leopold Labedz, eds., *Literature and Revolution in Soviet Russia, 1917-62* (London: Oxford University Press, 1963).

[13] Johnson, *op. cit.*, p. 21.

[14] See Carl A. Linden, *op. cit.*, pp. 146-173. Linden lists as the causes for the First Secretary's retreat: the Cuban missile crisis, *apparatchiki* resistance to the 1962 Party reorganization, and problems with China.

nomic line. The setback led to a reversal of the Party's cultural policy
as well. Leonid Ilichev, then a CC Secretary and chairman of the newly
formed Ideological Commission, led the attack at two special meetings
between the Party and creative writers, one in December 1962, the
other in March 1963.[15] Ilichev took a militant stand. Declaring that
there could be "no peaceful coexistence in art," he singled out Yevtushenko and Solzhenitsyn for criticism. The campaign peaked in 1963
with a barrage of criticism against Ilya Ehrenburg, Viktor Nekrasov,
Andrei Voznesensky, and the whole of the liberal wing. The conservatives made obvious gains, e.g., V. A. Kosolapov, the mildly liberal
editor of *Literaturnaya gazeta,* was fired (allegedly for having published Yevtushenko's "Babi Yar") and replaced by a former *Oktyabr*
editor, Alexander Chakovsky.

Thaws and freezes in Party-literary relations affect the factions dif-
ferently—a boon to one faction is the bane of the other. There is, however, an underlying unity of interests between the factions as well. Both
the liberals and conservatives are threatened by *apparatchiki* dominance over cultural affairs. As long as literature is so politically charged
Party leaders attempt to play one faction off the other. As a consequence both factions seek to influence Party policy. The trends for the
literary elite, therefore, give some measure of the extent to which the
Party's control over literature is weakening. Figure 6 illustrates the
trends of the literary elite.

Party-literary policy conflict exists in every sample year and reaches
significant proportions in 1955 and throughout the 1959-65 period for
a 24% increase in conflict over time. The key issues of contention concern elite socialization and the question of what the Party's role should
be. Literary participatory attitudes increase as well, moving from a 2.6
average in 1952-57 to a 3.2 (the "active interest group" range) in 1959-
65. Major trends over time support what many observers see as a weakening of the Party's mechanisms of literary control and the emergence
of Soviet writers as an active political force.[16]

---

[15] See Johnson, *op. cit.,* for an analysis of the two meetings, pp. 105-122, 137-186.
[16] Max Hayward, for example, summarizes the findings of an international sym-
posium on Soviet literature in the post-Stalin period with this observation:
   What are the gains made by the Soviet writers—and hence by the Soviet
   intelligensia as a whole—during the last ten years? Few would deny that in
   the process of their struggle—we sometimes forget how hard won these
   gains were—the writers have in practice achieved a greater degree of independence from Party control than any other group in the population. They
   have made literature a forum. . . . They have recently demonstrated . . .
   their capacity to resist attempts to re-impose on them the dead letter of a
   totally inane dogma. The Party tries to keep up appearances by continuing

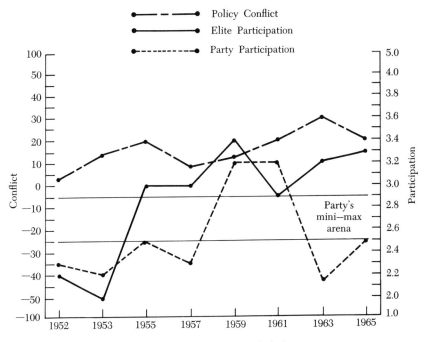

Fig. 6. Party-Literary Elite Relations

The years 1955-57 and 1963-65 are years of *apparatchiki*-literary elite crisis. In these years the Party demands a dominant role in the political arena (particularly in 1957 and 1963, both "freeze" years), only to meet with high levels of literary elite policy conflict and instrumental scores on the participatory categories. The conflict is appreciably greater in 1963-65 than in the earlier time of troubles as both the level of policy conflict and participatory demands are more firmly rooted in the instrumental range. In both 1963 and 1965 the Party backed away from the threatened general repression of the liberals and steered a middle course, apparently "torn between powerful conflicting trends and attempting to placate, or at least not to anagonize, violently opposed groups in Soviet society, if not in the party itself."[17]

As the data suggest, the conflict between the Party and literary elite seems irreconcilable—the *apparatchiki* demands dominance, the liter-

---

to present itself as the guardian of an increasingly ill-defined orthodoxy. But . . . 'the Party is defending an intellectual vacuum.' Everybody knows this and the King, in fact, is naked. "Epilogue," in Hayward and Crowley, *op. cit.*, p. 204.

[17] Max Hayward, ed., trans., *On Trial: The Soviet State versus Abram Tertz and Nikolai Arzhak* (New York: Harper and Row, 1966), p. 38.

ary greater independence from Party control. The 1966 trial of Sinyasky and Daniel did not alter the Party-literary elite relationship. If anything, tension increased, for the writers' reaction to the trial and harsh punishment was not submission, recantation, or a "conspiracy of silence," but open protest.[18]

V. Summary: Party-Specialist Elite Relations

Apparatchiki-Specialist relations in the post-Stalin period are competitive. Party-elite conflict—disputes over policy and conflict on the question of who should make policy decisions—pervade the Soviet political system. Specialist trends are charted in Figure 7.

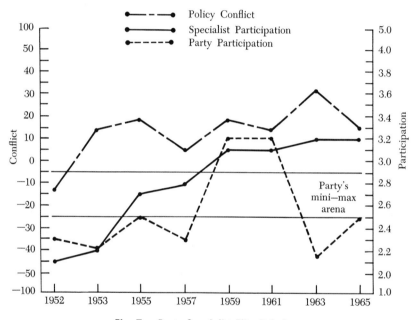

Fig. 7.   Party-Specialist Elite Relations

Apparatchiki-Specialist elite conflict is a continuous and crucial fact of the post-Stalin period. "The opposing tendencies between oligarchy and dictatorship" [here, elite participation and Party dominance] ap-

---

[18] See Timothy McClure, "The Politics of Soviet Culture, 1964-67," *Problems of Communism*, Vol. XVI, No. 2 (March-April 1967), pp. 26-43; Ronald Hingley, "Soviet Cultural Policy Since the 20th Party Congress," *Modern World*, Annual Review, 1965-66, pp. 20-30. Additional Support for this view may be found in the special issue, "In Quest of Justice," *Problems of Communism*, Vol. XVII, Nos. 4 and 5 (July-Aug. and Sept.-Oct., 1968).

pear to be the centrifugal forces of the post-Stalin period.[19] Over time all the specialist elites develop a participatory set of attitudes, an instrumental policy orientation, and show appreciable gains in group consciousness.

Insofar as Party-Specialist attitudes reflect the state of the Soviet political system, systemic trends are remarkably steady, progressing from a "satellite" system in 1952-53, to a "potential interest group" system from 1955 to 1957, and culminating in a participatory, "active interest group" system in the 1959-65 period. Throughout the later period, both the level of the elite participation and Party-Specialist policy conflict is in the "active-interest-group" range.

Specialist Attitudes	1959	1961	1963	1965
Participation	3.1	3.1	3.2	3.2
Policy	+27	+27	+37	+29

On a system-wide basis, then, *apparatchiki*-specialist elite attitudinal relations in the post-Stalin period are characterized by change—the erosion of attitudinal supports of Party dominance in the political system.

In sum, the Soviet political system is competitive. By 1959-65 participatory elite attitudes and Party-elite conflict reach levels which are incompatible with the ideological model. Party-specialist elite interdependence, not *apparatchiki* dominance, characterizes Party-elite relations. The trend is toward what may be tentatively termed a "polyarchical" system,[20] toward what H. Gordon Skilling calls a "pluralism of elites."[21] New models of Soviet politics, incorporating specialist elite participation, are obviously needed.[22] The Soviet political system, when conceived as a monolith, is a myth.

---

[19] Linden, *op. cit.*, p. 3, and throughout the Introduction, pp. 1-21.

[20] Robert A. Dahl, *Preface to Democratic Theory* (Chicago: University of Chicago Press, 1956), Chap. 3.

[21] "Interest Groups and Communist Politics," *World Politics*, XVIII, 3 (June, 1966), p. 449. For a suggestive analysis of elite pluralism see Robert A. Dahl and Charles E. Lindblom, *Politics, Economics, and Welfare* (New York: Harper Torchbooks, 1963), esp. the discussion of hierarchy, polyarchy, and bargaining, pp. 302-309.

[22] Alex Inkeles, "Models in the Analysis of Soviet Society," *Survey* No. 60 (July, 1966), pp. 3-12.

APPENDIX A *Instructions to Coders*

Content analysis is a research technique for the objective, systematic, and quantitative description of the manifest content of communication. Content analysis is objective to the extent that the dimensions are so precisely constructed that coders will record the same material in the same way. It is systematic in that all the material in the sample is analyzed along all the dimensions. Rounding out this overview, it is quantitative insofar as frequency-of-occurrence counts are tallied for each elite on every relevant dimension. The extent to which the study is systematic and objective determines the degree of reliability for the findings. Since two coders will independently code the same material, a measure of reliability can be calculated.

The analysis of manifest content, not esoteric or latent meanings, is significant only if a basic assumption is accepted, namely, that the frequency-of-occurrence of articulated values and beliefs is important, that the crucial values will be reiterated most often over time. The question of validity, whether or not the statements in the press represent the true positions of the elite, is moot—at this stage assumed, not proven. All articulated preferences and beliefs are treated as having equal weight.

116

The Sample

In this research project, five elites will be studied, each represented by its most influential journals and newspapers. Experts both here at the Institute and in the United States have agreed that the periodicals are representative, that is, the journals are written by and for the particular elite. The elites to be studied are:

The Party Apparat	Kommunist
	Partiinaya Zhizn
Economic Bureaucrats	Voprosy ekonomiki
	Ekonomicheskaya gazeta
Military	Krasnaya zvezda
Legal	Sovetskoye gosudarstvo i pravo
	Sovestskaya yustitsia
Literary	Novy mir
	Literaturnaya gazeta
	Oktyabr

We will read an equal number of paragraphs for each elite for the years 1952, 1953, 1955, 1957, 1959, 1961, 1963, 1965. All told, 600 paragraphs will be read for each elite per year, a total of 3,000 paragraphs per year for all five elites for a grand total of 24,000 paragraphs for the entire study.

Reliability

To guarantee that we are reading and coding the periodicals accurately, a method has been devised to check agreement between us. All articles will be coded separately by two coders working independently. Although this increases our work, it allows us to gain confidence in our analysis of the articles. [In fact, 25% of all articles were recoded. The coders were purposely misled on this issue.]

A commonsensical method for determining how well we understand the categories and how accurately we code the material has been devised for the study. Suppose, for example, that two coders, A and B, separately read the same article of 50 paragraphs. Coder A found 9 paragraphs which applied to the questions, while coder B believes 11 are applicable. When compared, they agree, let us say, on 8. Thus, we calculate agreement by dividing the total number of disagreements, 4, 1 + 3, by their total agreements in the article, 46, for 92 percent agreement. When we reach 80% agreement our findings may be considered reliable and our practice session will end, although this reliability-checking system will continue throughout the whole study.

Selection of articles

The articles to be read were chosen according to the following criteria:

(a) We will read the *first signed article* in the selected journals. We will not read the introductory piece, "Progressive," in journals, since these merely give the Party line, and we are reading Party journals to find Party values.

(b) On your Code Sheet will be written the name and issue of the periodicals to be read, as well as the pages to be read. Read only the number of pages written on the Code Sheet, for it is of utmost importance that we read the same amount of material for each elite each year.*

(c) The issues of each periodical to be read each year varies. This is called "staggered start sampling" and is done to insure against some inclusion or exclusion of authors, values, or topics. Thus, e.g., in 1955, we took the first 10 pages of the lead signed article of every fourth issue of *Kommunist* and *Partiinnaya zhizn* for each year, an average of 300 paragraphs for each journal for an average of 600 paragraphs each elite.

Coding Procedures

General coding instructions

1. The basic unit of analysis is the paragraph.

2. An item which *clearly* relates to one of the Value Dimensions is to be coded if it is the basic value or belief—the major theme—expressed in that paragraph and not merely a passing reference.

3. No more than one value may be recorded per paragraph. You must select the major theme.

4. Many values may be recorded per article, even if contradictory to other recorded values or repetitions, since we are interested in how often a value is expressed.

---

* The number of pages to be read for each journal was calculated as follows. The average number of paragraphs per page for each journal was counted. By dividing the number of paragraphs into the total number of our sample for each year (600 paragraphs per elite) we calculated the average number of pages which would equal this number of paragraphs. A similar process was followed in determining what articles were to be read in the newspapers and how many newspaper articles equal the number of pages in the journal.

5. Do not read the first or last paragraphs of an article, since these are traditionally homilies of loyalty to the Party.

Specific coding instructions

1. You will have a list of all the Value Dimensions for easy reference while reading the material.

2. You will also have a code sheet for each article you read. The code sheet is an outline of all the Dimensions and possible positions within each dimension. There is space beside each position for you to note the number of times that any of the values of beliefs are clearly articulated.

3. When, during the course of reading an article, you come upon a paragraph which has a major theme that clearly relates to one of the Dimensions (A, AA, B, etc.) carefully determine which position it fits (1, 2, 3, 4, 5, etc.).

4. Once the decision is made, note in the appropriate space beside the position the *page* and *paragraph* in which the major theme occurs. This notation must be exact so that we can later compare the results between the two coders who have read the article and determine the percentage of agreement. The notation system is simple. For example, 1/6 means page 1, paragraph 6, the slash (/) separating page from paragraph. A comma will be written after the paragraph number to separate one notation from another, 1/6, 2/4, 2/5, 2/6, etc.

5. Count paragraphs by beginning with the first paragraph of the article, or when over one page long with the first paragraph of the page. Thus, if you found a relevant theme in the fourth paragraph of page seven, you would write 7/4.

6. When you encounter a theme which you believe is very important, code it in the appropriate space, then, to call attention to its importance, bracket it. For example, (7/6) means page 7 paragraph 6 is especially important.

APPENDIX B *The Coders*

In content analysis the successful collection of reliable data depends in large part on the coders—on their intelligence, mastery of the coding instructions and categories, perseverance, and commitment.[1] The five coders for the project had been employed primarily as translators and Russian language teachers at the Institute for the Study of the USSR in Munich. All were Russian emigres who had left the Soviet Union before World War II. Their backgrounds were varied—one a former professor of History at the University of Kiev, another a retired Red Army colonel, a third an assistant editor of a West German journal on Soviet economics, another a former Russian language instructor at Stanford University, the last a full-time translator. Two others went through the training period but, unable to analyze the material with a sufficiently high level of reliability, returned to positions as translators.

Numerous steps were taken to insure inter-coder reliability. Since the categories were "frozen" following the pretest stage,[2] training ses-

---

[1] C.f., Dorwin P. Cartwright, "Analysis of Qualitative Material" in Leon Festinger and Daniel Katz, eds., *Research Methods in the Behavioral Sciences* (New York: Holt, Rinehart and Winston, 1953), pp. 461-466.

[2] A "Round Robin" procedure, similar to that used by the Institute for Social Research at the University of Michigan, was utilized throughout the pretest stage

sions focused on mastering the technique. The training period lasted for four weeks, five hours a day, five days a week. Training included:

(1) a general discussion of the method;

(2) a thorough discussion of the categories and positions;

(3) practice sessions using illustrative material derived from the pretest, especially problematical paragraphs;

(4) practice coding on journals, not using the articles from the sample, followed by discussions of paragraphs which were not coded the same by the coders. Not until the fourth week of training (ninety hours of instruction and practice per coder) did the reliability tests reach the desired level and the project begin.

Several procedures were adopted to minimize coder subjectivity, some of which have already been discussed above, e.g., dealing with manifest content and not esoteric language or latent intentions. Of special importance was the decision to avoid a full explanation of the project's hypotheses; thus, no mention was made of trend analysis. To insure against the coder's discovery of intent, elite journals, sample articles, and years were "mixed"; that is, no coder concentrated on any elite, or journal, or year. This was another precaution against systematic coder bias. It also reinforced the decision to read manifest content by ruling out the possibility of any coder becoming a "specialist" on an elite.

To further guard against coder subjectivity, the coders were told that only those paragraphs for which there was inter-coder reliability were to be tabulated. This was untrue, done to counter the psychological "reward" inherent in content analysis to find codable material in the content. By emphasizing the need for coding only clearly articulated preferences, the "reward" system was reversed, changing the focus from quantity to quality control. This was made possible by the fact that during the practice sessions inter-coder agreement was checked daily and disagreements discussed. Pay was in no way related to quantity. Group rewards for high reliability developed and worked extremely well.

---

and later for training project coders. A set of articles was collected and each coder coded the material independently. All disagreements among coders were noted and used as a check on the reliability of coding. On the basis of these disagreements, categories and positions were rewritten. The pretest ended when a high level of intercoder reliability was attained. These categories and positions were then frozen for the project's coding.

APPENDIX C *Saliency on The Participatory Categories*

CATEGORY I. Policy-making is the responsibility of

	1952	1953	1955	1957	1959	1961	1963	1965
Party	7	12	9	15	11	11	13	18
Economic	0	8	23	13	15	10	19	21
Legal	0	6	8	12	8	13	9	14
Military	—	—	14	23	0	11	25	16
Literary	9	7	8	17	7	8	11	13

CATEGORY II. Policy-making should be the responsibility of

	1952	1953	1955	1957	1959	1961	1963	1965
Party	5	12	19	21	14	16	30	29
Economic	11	12	21	17	10	18	23	27
Legal	6	11	16	18	14	19	25	22
Military	—	—	16	24	3	7	27	18
Literary	5	7	18	14	16	18	20	26

CATEGORY III. Decision-making is the responsibility of

	1952	1953	1955	1957	1959	1961	1963	1965
Party	8	16	29	27	24	26	26	21
Economic	0	12	25	12	22	16	23	26
Legal	8	0	12	11	10	14	12	12
Military	—	—	17	26	12	15	22	19
Literary	5	6	17	9	15	7	18	14

CATEGORY IV. Decision-making should be the responsibility of

	1952	1953	1955	1957	1959	1961	1963	1965
Party	9	14	27	29	24	28	20	25
Economic	10	12	25	10	31	21	33	41
Legal	6	8	13	13	16	17	14	15
Military	—	—	19	26	17	15	16	14
Literary	11	6	14	12	16	17	11	12

CATEGORY V. Justifications for policy recommendations

	1952	1953	1955	1957	1959	1961	1963	1965
Party	11	15	17	23	20	22	24	23
Economic	9	10	20	14	19	17	26	23
Legal	4	7	10	16	13	15	19	15
Military	—	—	12	14	6	8	14	15
Literary	5	6	8	13	12	10	12	12

Bibliography

Books

Almond, Gabriel, and G. Bingham Powell, Jr., *Comparative Politics: A Developmental Approach*. Boston: Little, Brown & Co., 1967.

Azrael, Jeremy, *Managerial Power and Soviet Politics*. Cambridge: Harvard University Press, 1966.

Brzezinski, Zbigniew, and Samuel Huntington, *Political Power: USA/USSR*. New York: The Viking Press, Inc., 1964.

Dahl, Robert A., *A Preface to Democratic Theory*. Chicago: University of Chicago Press, 1956.

——————, *Who Governs: Democracy and Power in an American City*. New Haven, Conn.: Yale University Press, 1961.

——————, and Charles E. Lindblom, *Politics, Economics, and Welfare*. New York: Harper & Row, Publishers, 1963.

Eisenstadt, S. N., *The Political Systems of Empires*. New York: The Free Press, 1963.

Fainsod, Merle, *How Russia is Ruled*. 2d ed. Cambridge, Mass.: Harvard University Press, 1963.

124

Festinger, Leon, and Daniel Katz, *Research Methods in the Behavioral Sciences.* New York: Holt, Rinehart and Winston, 1953.

Gripp, Richard C., *Patterns of Soviet Politics.* Homewood, Illinois: Dorsey Press, 1967.

Hayward, Max, ed., trans. *On Trial: The Soviet State versus Abram Tertz and Nikolai Arzhak.* New York: Harper & Row, Publishers, 1966.

——————, and Edward Crowley, eds. *Soviet Literature in the Sixties.* New York: Frederick A. Praeger, Inc., 1964.

——————, and Leopold Labedz, eds. *Literature and Revolution in Soviet Russia, 1917-62.* London: Oxford University Press, 1963.

Johnson, Priscilla, *Khrushchev and the Arts: The Politics of Soviet Culture, 1962-1964.* Cambridge: M.I.T. Press, 1965.

Kassov, Allen, *Prospects For Soviet Society.* New York: Frederick A. Praeger, Inc., 1968.

Keller, Suzanne, *Beyond the Ruling Class: Strategic Elites in Modern Society.* New York: Random House, 1963.

Kolkowicz, Roman, *The Soviet Military and the Communist Party.* Princeton: Princeton University Press, 1967.

Linden, Carl, *Khrushchev and the Soviet Leadership, 1957-1964.* Baltimore: Johns Hopkins University Press, 1966.

Moore, Barrington, *Terror and Progress—USSR: Some Sources of Change and Stability in the Soviet Dictatorship.* New York: Harper & Row, Publishers, 1954.

Ploss, Sidney, *Conflict and Decision-Making in Soviet Russia: A Case Study of Agricultural Policy, 1953-1963.* Princeton, N.J.: Princeton University Press, 1967.

Pye, Lucian W., and Sidney Verba. *Political Culture and Political Development.* Princeton, N.J.: Princeton University Press, 1965.

Ritvo, Herbert, *The New Soviet Society.* New York: The New Leader, 1962.

Stewart, Philip D., *Political Power in the Soviet Union.* New York: The Bobbs-Merrill Co., Inc., 1968.

Truman, David, *The Governmental Process: Political Interests and Public Opinion.* New York: Alfred A. Knopf, 1958.

Wolfe, Thomas, *Soviet Strategy at the Crossroads.* Cambridge, Mass.: Harvard University Press, 1964.

Articles

Angell, Robert, "Social Values of Soviet and American Elites," *Journal of Conflict Resolution,* VII, 4 (December, 1964), 330-385.

Barghoorn, Frederick C., "Soviet Political Doctrine and the Problem of Opposition," *Bucknell Review,* XII (May, 1964), 1-29.

Barry, Donald B., "The Specialist in Soviet Policy-Making: The Adoption of a Law," *Soviet Studies,* XVI, 2 (October, 1964), 152-165.

Berman, Harold, "The Struggle of Soviet Jurists Against a Return to Stalinist Terror," *Slavic Review,* XXII, 2 (June, 1963), 314-320.

Dennis, Jack, "Major Problems of Political Socialization Research," *Midwest Journal of Political Science,* XII, 1 (February, 1968), 85-114.

Dunham, Vera S., "Insights from Soviet Literature," *Journal of Conflict Resolution,* VIII, 4 (December, 1964), 386-410.

Eckstein, Harry, "Group Theory and the Comparative Study of Pressure Groups," in Harry Eckstein and David Apter, eds., *Comparative Politics: A Reader.* New York: The Free Press, 1963, 389-397.

Editorial. "Concerning Discussions in Scholarly Journals," *Kommunist,* No. 7, 1955, 1-10.

Fleron, Frederic, Jr., "The Soviet Political Elite: Aspects of Political and Economic Development in the USSR," Paper presented at the 1968 Annual Meeting of the American Political Science Association, Washington, D.C., September 2-7, 1968.

Gallagher, Matthew P., "Military Manpower: A Case Study," *Problems of Communism,* XVI, 2 (May-June, 1964), 53-62.

Gehlen, Michael, "Group Theory and the Study of Soviet Politics," University of California, Berkeley, monograph.

Grzybowski, Kazimierz, "Soviet Criminal Law," *Problems of Communism,* XIV, 2 (March-April, 1965), 53-62.

Hingley, Ronald, "Soviet Cultural Policy since the 20th Party Congress," *Modern World,* Annual Review, 1965-66, 20-30.

Inkeles, Alex, "Models in the Analysis of Soviet Society," *Survey,* No. 60 (July, 1966), 3-12.

Lowenthal, Robert, "The Logic of One-Party Rule," *Problems of Communism,* VII, 2 (March-April, 1958), 21-30.

McClure, Timothy, "The Politics of Soviet Culture, 1964-67," *Problems of Communism,* XVI, 2 (March-April, 1967), 26-43.

Schwartz, Joel J., and William R. Keech, "Group Influence on the Policy Process in the Soviet Union," *American Political Science Review,* LXIII, No. 3 (September, 1968), 840-851.

Skilling, H. Gordon, "Interest Groups and Communist Politics," *World Politics,* XVIII, 3 (June, 1966), 435-451.

Singer, J. David, "Social Values and Foreign Policy Attitudes of Soviet and American Elites," *Journal of Conflict Resolution*, VIII, 4 (December, 1964), 411-491.

Special Issue. "Law and Legality in the USSR," *Problems of Communism*, XIV, 2 (March-April, 1965).

Special Issues. "In Quest of Justice," *Problems of Communism*, XVII, Nos. 4 and 5 (July-August and September-October, 1968).

Tannenbaum, Percy H., and Jade M. McLeod, "On the Measurement of Socialization," *Public Opinion Quarterly*, XXXI, I (Spring, 1967), 27-37.

Tregub, Semion, "Report to the Eighth Plenum of the Russian Writers' Union," *Literaturnaya Rossiia*, No. 15 (April 12), 1963, 1.

INDEX

Index